T0357947

Starting with
SHARES

Starting with
SHARES

A BEGINNER'S GUIDE
TO SHAREMARKET SUCCESS

Roger Kinsky

WILEY

First published in 2022 by John Wiley & Sons Australia, Ltd
42 McDougall St, Milton Qld 4064
Office also in Melbourne

Typeset in Liberation Serif 11pt/14pt

© John Wiley & Sons Australia, Ltd 2022

The moral rights of the author have been asserted

ISBN: 978-0-730-39516-4

A catalogue record for this
book is available from the
National Library of Australia

Cover design by Wiley
Cover Image: © Miloje/Shutterstock

Illustration sketches and concepts by Roger Kinsky
Illustrations by Delia Sala/Wiley

Disclaimer

Printed in Singapore
M118105_111021

Contents

Introduction

Australians have traditionally been interested in shares as a viable way of investing over the longer term and also making profits in the shorter term. Share ownership is ever growing and a recent study showed that about 6.6 million Australian adults, or 35 per cent of the population, own shares. In the past, share investing was often seen as the domain of males, but more recently there's been a growing trend for women to get involved and nowadays almost half our share investors are women. At the same time, there's been an emerging trend for younger people to get into shares. Investors today are also growing more interested in a wider diversity of shares in different asset classes, including international shares. In short, Australians from all walks of life are becoming more involved with a wider variety of shares.

The growing interest in shares is partly driven by low interest rates, which make holding cash in a bank account or term deposit a really unattractive proposition. At the same time, Australian property is increasingly more expensive and slipping out of the reach of many Australians. Shares are a viable investment alternative because you don't need a lot of money to get going. In fact, you can become a shareholder with as little as $500.

Unfortunately, many would-be investors don't know a great deal about shares and so lack the confidence to plunge into the sharemarket. If you fall into this category, this book is definitely for you! To make the book as user-friendly as possible, I try to avoid jargon unless the term is in common usage. In this case, I try to explain it in a straightforward manner that I hope will be readily understandable. I've minimised the complications of share investing by outlining only those strategies that I believe are really important for your success. In addition, I've provided heaps of tips that

I hope you'll find useful. These are simply my suggestions, not as an infallible investment guru, but as someone who has learned about shares from my successes — and failures — over 50-plus years of share investing.

You'll find the book contains many simple illustrations. These are often in a light-hearted vein and are aimed to help reinforce your understanding of an important point. They may also help you to look at an issue affecting shares in a somewhat new (and hopefully useful) light. All illustrations were re-drawn from my original sketches by illustrator, Delia Sala.

This book complements my other share investing books, also published by Wiley Australia:

- *Online Investing on the Australian Sharemarket*, 5th edition

- *Teach Yourself about Shares*, 3rd edition

- *Shares Made Simple*

- *Charting Made Simple.*

The publishers and I have taken every precaution to make this book free of errors and typos but perfection is extremely difficult to attain. In a book of over 50 000 words, a few errors or typos will inevitably slip through. If you notice any of these, I would be most grateful to hear from you. I'm always happy to receive feedback or suggestions from readers so if you have any comments please contact me at: rkinsky@bigpond.com. I'll make every effort to answer all emails within a day or two of receiving them.

You can also visit my website, rogerkinskyshares.com.au, for further discussion about shares and my books. The site features a weekly blog 'Sharing shares', where I discuss topical items of interest to share investors. I also offer a share mentoring and education service, where I can help you with any difficulties you may experience. Details on how to access this service are outlined on my website.

Finally, I wish you a profitable share investing experience and I trust that this book will play a significant role in guiding you on your path to success with shares.

Roger Kinsky
Woollamia, NSW
October 2021

Chapter 1

What you need to know

In this chapter, I outline what you really need to know about investing in shares so you can get started, covering market unpredictability, the relationship between risk and reward, and what you're actually investing in when you buy shares. I also highlight some of the stuff you don't really need. Are you surprised at that? You might think that the more you know about shares, the greater the profit you'll make when you invest in them. Actually, no evidence indicates that 'more' information is necessarily better; in fact, 'more' can be worse because you can get bogged down in detail and miss the important stuff. And, as I explain, some great share investing strategies are based on very simple ideas that anyone can apply.

Before I go too much further, however, I'd like you to meet someone who you'll see a lot of through this book.

Meet Michelle

In most cases, when financial decisions are involved a bias exists toward the male gender. Company directors and top executives are still predominantly male. And most finance books still seem to assume that the reader is male.

'Hi! I'm Michelle. I'll be accompanying you on your journey.'

In this book, I try to avoid gender discrimination and, because of the current bias toward males, I have deliberately used a female named Michelle in my illustrations. She appears in most of the illustrations in this book, guiding you through your introduction to share investing.

Sorry fellas, I have nothing against the male gender but women are fast becoming a force in the financial arena. By the way, studies have shown that when it comes to share investing, women are more successful than men. I explain why in chapter 5.

Trust yourself

When it comes to share investing, I want you to trust yourself and not think you need to rely on others such as share investment advisors. Many people feel like 'dunces' when it comes to share investing—even those with a good education. This means people often rely on investment advisors or share advisors who they believe are experts in the field—and who usually charge a hefty fee for service.

However, from my own personal experience, acquired over 50-odd years of share investing, I have found that the results don't always justify the cost. In fact, my most disastrous share investments occurred as a result of following recommendations. Now I no longer act on advice without first putting it through the 'grist of the mill of my own mind' and coming to my own conclusions.

I wrote this book so I could explain the basic principles of share investing in a way you can understand so you won't need to seek 'expert' advice. Believe me, most ordinary people have the necessary nous to be successful share investors once they grasp the basic principles. If you ignore the hype and jargon, 'it really ain't that hard'. You won't always be right and not all your share investments will be profitable, but you can take heart in the fact that no person and no computer program can make profitable predictions about shares that are always right.

Knowledge level you'll need

I have written many non-fiction books over the past 50 years, and taught many classes on subjects ranging from engineering theory to shares. When I start teaching a new class or writing a new book, I face the difficulty of determining the knowledge level of the students or readers who want to learn. If I pitch the starting point too high, those who don't have the pre-requisite knowledge get lost at the start and have to try to catch up. But starting from behind isn't a good idea when learning a new skill or acquiring new knowledge because you have to learn the old stuff at the same time as you are trying to absorb the new.

On the other hand, if I pitch the beginning point too low, those who already know a fair bit get bored and can easily lose interest. After all, if someone is going to learn something new they need to be interested.

'How am I going to catch up?'

My publishers and I decided to pitch this book about shares at the beginner level—which explains the title 'Starting with Shares'. I've been faithful to the title and assumed you know very little about shares, and have made that my starting point. You can find plenty of books about shares and lots of info is available on the internet, but the problem with most of these sources is that they usually assume the reader already knows a fair bit about shares—certainly enough to understand the terminology. In this book, I explain everything in a way that you can understand even if you know virtually nothing about shares. As far as possible, I avoid the use

of jargon—although I do have to use some of the terms commonly used with shares because you need to understand them to find your way. But before I use a term that might be unfamiliar to you, I explain it first in everyday, straightforward language.

If you already know a fair bit about shares, you may want to skim over some of the content in the early chapters. But there's an inherent danger in this that I now discuss.

Types of knowledge

Knowledge comes in several types. One type is the knowledge you know you don't know. For example, you may be aware that you don't know much about servicing or repairing a car. So when your car needs servicing or has some problem, you take it to a mechanic who has the required knowledge and can service or repair your car. But there may also be a whole mountain of knowledge out there that you don't know you don't know. This is called *blissful ignorance*, because you don't worry about things you don't know about. For example, your car could have a fault that you're not aware of and so you keep driving the car until the fault gets worse. One day you notice the problem and take your car to your mechanic. The mechanic may say something like, 'Well, if you had brought the car in to me earlier I could have fixed the problem easily and cheaply, but now it's a big and expensive fix'. The reason you didn't bring the car in earlier was because you weren't aware of the problem.

When it comes to shares, you may be aware of your lack of knowledge in certain areas but you might also have a lack of knowledge in areas you're not even aware of and that might cause problems.

Finally, there is knowledge you think you know but really don't—and this can be very dangerous. For example, when I first bought a yacht and started cruising, the yacht once ran aground during the night. I'd thought

I knew how to anchor a yacht safely but, in fact, I wasn't following the best procedure at all and when the wind changed unexpectedly while I was asleep I ended up in trouble.

That's why I suggest you don't fast-forward through the early chapters without at least skim reading first to ensure you aren't skipping over something you really don't understand.

How long is the journey?

You're probably wondering how far we're going to go and what you really need to know so you'll be able to make a success of share investing. You can access a whole heap of info about shares — in fact, I reckon you could spend the rest of your life going through what's available and you still wouldn't have touched all of it.

'How can I hope to compete?'

If you try to learn too much, you can easily become overwhelmed and reach the point where you do virtually nothing — known as *paralysis by analysis*. So I'm not going to try to take you to an advanced knowledge level about shares. If I tried to do this, the book would end up being a tome and you'd be deterred right from the start. So I'm going to take you only as far as you need to go to become a successful share investor. You can acquire the rest as you get into shares, or if you're sufficiently interested, you can obtain more advanced knowledge later on.

The really heartening news is that you don't actually need to be very savvy on all aspects of share investing to be a profitable share investor. Some really simple and successful strategies have been devised that focus on only a few key issues. If you are faced with a choice of strategies, I suggest you choose a simple one in preference to a complex one that requires heaps of information or the use of sophisticated computer algorithms.

Tip

If you get to the point where you want to expand your knowledge about shares, I can recommend the following books. Naturally I can recommend them because I wrote them!

- *Teach Yourself about Shares*, 3rd edition
- *Online Investing on the Australian Sharemarket*, 5th edition
- *Shares Made Simple*
- *Charting Made Simple*

Markets are unpredictable

You might think that the more you learn about shares, the better you'll be able to predict how the market or a particular share will perform. A friend of mine who's knowledgeable about shares recently told me he had sold all his shares because he was sure that after the market recovered from the downturns caused by the COVID-19 pandemic, it would dive again. Guess what? The market kept rising and reached new heights.

The sharemarket is difficult to predict basically because *people* buy and sell shares and it's very difficult to predict how a person will react in a certain situation. So imagine the difficulty in trying to predict how thousands will react to situations on the sharemarket that change all the time. Another complicating factor is that people have an instinctive tendency towards 'herd' behaviour, ingrained over thousands of years of human evolution. This instinct tends to make them want to take safety in numbers and 'follow the leader'—so just a few people acting in a certain way can influence others to also act in the same way. Different strategies can work in different situations, and no one strategy works well in all situations. No 'magic bullet' exists with shares. Ignore anyone—including a respected share authority or advisor—who tells you they have a system with shares that succeeds in all situations. Especially walk away if they want you to part with a sizeable heap of your hard-earned money to gain access to this super-duper system.

You might argue that computers can be programmed to trade shares and computers don't make mistakes. That's true but the fact that computers don't make mistakes doesn't mean they can predict the future with any degree of certainty. Computers need programs and those programs have to be written by a person. They will reflect the programmer's preferences and experiences and, therefore, still operate with in-built biases.

Tip

The uncertainty and unpredictability of shares actually works in your favour because they mean you can be as good as anyone else. You don't need to pay advisors and you don't need to buy an expensive computer program to make a success of share investing. All you really need is an understanding of how the sharemarket operates and how to access the info you need. After you've read through this book, you should have that knowledge—and then it's up to you to apply it to your best advantage.

Dealing with the uncertainty

I don't want to give you the impression that because of the uncertainty involved with shares, learning about them or applying strategies in different situations is pointless. When you're operating in an uncertain environment, the trick is to swing the probabilities in your favour. That's really what this book is about—helping you to adopt strategies that will improve your chance of success in the various situations you'll encounter with the sharemarket.

Because of the uncertainty with shares a certain strategy may work well in some cases, but the opposite strategy might also work! Let's look at an example. Consider the following two strategies:

- *Strategy 1:* Buy shares that are at the top of their 12-month price range. The reasoning behind this strategy could be, 'The share price has been rising and that's a good sign. If the price rise continues, I'll make a good profit by buying the shares now'.

- *Strategy 2:* Buy shares that are at around the bottom of their 12-month price range. The reasoning here could be, 'If the share price has bottomed and starts to rise again, I'll make good profits because I'm getting in at the ground floor'.

You can see that each strategy is different but each can be justified with a logical argument. And if you apply them, you might find that each one results in good profits! For example, you may buy some shares that are at the top of their 12-month price range and find that their price continues to rise so you make a good profit. At the same time, you could buy some shares that are around the bottom of their price range and find that they stage a turnaround and the price rises and you also make a good profit on them.

This is because with different shares in different situations one strategy might be better than another. So no single strategy is necessarily best in every situation and able to produce good results every time.

Tip

The strategy of looking for shares trading at around their low price and that have a good chance of rising is known as *bottom fishing*.

Here's another example of two very different ways of choosing shares:

- *Strategy 1:* Choose an investment mix of 10 shares by careful analysis and research based on all the available information about them you can access.

- *Strategy 2:* Choose a share to invest in by pinning a share listing on a soft board and throwing a dart at it. Do this 10 times to get an investment mix of 10 different shares.

Tip

Throwing darts at a share listing pinned to a board isn't really practical, but choosing a mix of shares by random selection is certainly possible. Choosing shares by random selection is still known as a *dart* or *dartboard* approach.

Some time ago I tried each of these two strategies to see the result. I chose a mix of 10 shares based on my research and I chose another mix using a selection process based on random numbers. I wrote down the shares each strategy had indicated and their current price. Some time later I checked the share prices and worked out the profit or loss each strategy had produced.

Guess what? Each strategy resulted in a profitable investment and, in fact, the dart approach was slightly superior to the careful selection approach!

When I pointed this out in a share investing course, one student responded with a simple question: *'If that's so, why am I wasting my time and money doing this course?'*

I admit this question floored me for a while and I couldn't really think of a reasonable answer. As I pondered on it, I came to realise a fundamental truth about share investing that this question had highlighted. Despite what most people think, choosing shares in the first place is really not the most important consideration for successful share investing. What really matters is what you do with the shares after you've bought them—that is, your management plan. I'll expand on management plans in chapter 11 but for now I'd like you to remember that you need a management plan if you're going to be a successful share investor.

My experiment also showed that although the dart approach is based on random selection, it can result in a good mix of shares because it's likely to give you a varied selection of many different types of shares. Having a varied mix of different types of shares is known as *diversification*, and is a strategy I'll expand on in later chapters. The real benefit of a dart approach is that it overcomes personal prejudice. We all have in-built preferences based on a combination of hereditary and environmental factors that we often aren't even aware of and which affect our decisions and actions. With share selection, they're likely to bias our selection process in one way or another. For example, you may have had your fingers burnt in the past with certain shares or certain types of shares and so may now have a 'once bitten, twice shy' bias toward these shares.

The main takeaway here is that it's important to build a selection of diversified shares and it's even more important to manage them successfully.

Tip

I expand on psychological factors relevant to share investing in later chapters.

Risk and reward are related

A really important principle of investing is that risk and reward are related. Reward with investing is the amount of profit you're likely to make. In most cases, as the potential reward increases, so too does the risk. Figure 1.1 shows shows the hypothetical relationship between risk and reward.

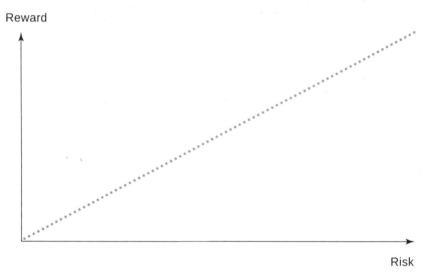

Figure 1.1: Increasing your possible reward usually means increased risk

The 'safer' an investment, the less risk is involved and so the less profit you can expect. I'm sure you already have a fundamental understanding of this relationship and that is why you want to get into shares. You realise that share investing involves more risk than a comparatively safe investment such as a bank deposit but the compensation for taking the higher risk is that the rewards can be greater. You also understand that you need to take the higher risk to reap the reward of a higher potential profit.

Shareholders are owners of a business

When you become a shareholder you're investing in a business. In fact, you become a part owner of that business. So what's a business? A business is a commercial enterprise that provides a product or service to consumers and usually aims to make a profit. (A non-profit-making business can be set up for charitable purposes but this is rare for Australian companies with listed shares.) You can't be a shareholder in businesses such as partnerships and private (or proprietary) companies unless invited to do so by the directors. The most common type of business in which you can be a shareholder is the public company.

As you might guess, a public company is a type of business where anyone can become a part-owner. It follows that the company has no control over who the owners are. Larger companies are also known as *corporations*.

The company has a separate legal identity from the owners and is regarded as a separate entity at law. This is known as a *body corporate* and means that the company can act very much as a person can in business situations. For example, the company owns assets and has liabilities (debts). It can enter into contracts such as contracts for employment or for the purchase of goods or services. Because of the separate legal identity, the assets of the owners are immune from the assets of the company.

So if you're a shareholder in a company, no matter how much financial difficulty the company may get itself into, your personal assets can't be used to pay creditors or to help bail the company out. In extreme cases, you could lose the money you've invested in their shares but that's the limit of your liability. A public company often uses the abbreviation 'Ltd' at the end of the name to indicate the limited liability of the owners.

Tip

BHP (Broken Hill Proprietary) is a well-known Australian public company with issued shares. The term *proprietary* is normally used to indicate a private company (that is, belonging to a proprietor or proprietors), as in 'Pty Ltd'. When BHP changed from a private to a public company, it obtained special exemption to retain 'proprietary' in the name because 'BHP' was so widely recognised by Australians.

Key takeaways

- I assume you don't have a good knowledge of shares and need to start from square one.

- With share investment strategies, it's generally better to err on the side of simplicity rather than complexity and keep in mind that simple strategies often work as well as complex ones.

- You don't have to know a heap about shares for them to be a profitable investment for you.

- The sharemarket has an inherent element of unpredictability associated with it.

- No share investing strategy works in every situation and there's certainly no magic bullet.

- Risk and reward are closely related; if you want a higher profit, you need to accept that a higher risk will be involved.

- Most companies aim to make a profit from the sale of a product or service.

- While many types of legal business structures are possible in Australia, the main structure applicable to shares is the limited company. If the shares are listed on an exchange, they can be purchased by anyone so this type of company is also known as a *public company*.

Chapter 2

Getting into shares

In this chapter, I discuss some of the basics about investing in shares, starting with some common terms you're likely to encounter. I then look at the different ways you can come to own shares and so become a share investor, and consider shares you can invest in as well as those you can't. I also explain why share prices change and the most commonly quoted prices. This will set the groundwork so you have a good foundation to work from as you get more into shares.

What are shares?

As discussed in chapter 1, shareholders are the owners of a company and, as the name suggests, a share is one unit of ownership. This means that someone with 10 000 shares owns a 10 times greater slice than someone with 1000 shares. As part-owners, shareholders are entitled to a share of the assets and profits

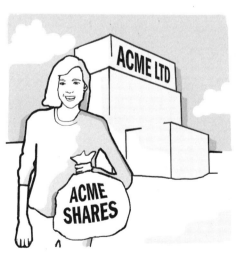

'Whoopee! I'm now a part owner of ACME LTD.'

of the business. They're also entitled to other benefits of ownership in a business enterprise, including having a say in the management of the business by attending annual general meetings (AGMs), asking questions and voting. Because a shareholder has equity in the business, shares are also called *equities*.

Understanding some basics

The following are some common terms you're likely to encounter as you start investing in shares. Some of them are a bit 'jargony', but understanding them is necessary as you progress along your journey.

Common share investing terms include:

- *Bulls and bears:* These terms have been around for a long time and no-one is exactly sure how they came about. Bulls are optimists who believe the market will rise and, therefore, they want to buy shares, whereas bears are pessimists who believe the market will fall and, therefore, want to sell shares.

- *Capital:* This is just a fancy word for money used in business.

- *Portfolio:* Your portfolio is the total of the shares you own. Your portfolio value changes as share prices change, so you can know its value only at a certain point in time. Your portfolio value also changes if the number of shares changes. The value rises if you add more shares and falls if you sell some of the shares you currently own.

- *Securities:* A security is a tradeable financial asset. Because shares have value and are tradeable, shares are one form of security. Many other types of security are available, including property, bonds and cash.

- *Securities exchange:* Shares are traded on a securities exchange (previously known as a *stock exchange*). Before a company can be listed with an exchange (and in order to remain listed) the company needs to satisfy stringent requirements of the exchange, the Australian Tax Office (ATO) and Australian financial laws that are enforced by ASIC (Australian Securities and Investments

Commission). If the company can jump through these hoops, and pay the required fees, it can be listed with the exchange and traded on their market. The company is now a listed public company. (I discuss this process in a little more detail in the section 'Making shares available for trading', later in this chapter.)

- *Share registry:* Most listed companies in Australia can't be bothered keeping track of the details of all their shareholders, because it's fiddley work and isn't really part of the business strengths of the company. So companies usually farm the shareholder work out to a share registry. This is an organisation set up to do precisely that—keep records of the details of all shareholders and their shareholding. Australia has several share registries, of which the most widely used ones are Computershare and Link Market Services. You can easily find out which share registry the company uses because it will be stated on any shareholder communication you receive.

- *Stocks:* This is just another name for shares and is often used to mean the total of the shares owned in a company. Don't get confused with 'stock', which refers to goods kept on hand by the business—that is, the materials or partly finished or finished products owned by a business. In this book, I mostly use the word 'shares' but sometimes I use 'stock', particularly when referring to all the shares in a company.

- *Stockmarket:* The trading market for shares is, naturally enough, known as the *stockmarket* or *sharemarket*. In Australia, the largest market is the Australian Securities Exchange (ASX) and it is most likely the one you'll use, but a number of smaller exchanges are also in operation.

- *Trading:* Trading is the process of purchasing or selling shares.

- *Trading hours:* As you might expect, an exchange isn't open for trading on a 24/7 basis. In Australia, the opening hours are 10 am to 4 pm, Monday to Friday, with the exchange closed on public holidays. Nowadays, you can place orders with many brokers outside of exchange trading hours but the order can't transact until the exchange is open for trading.

Tip

If you have any queries related to your shareholding or your dividend payments, trying to contact the company is pointless. Instead you need to contact the share registry or your broker, so keeping track of the share registry used by each of the companies you own shares in is worthwhile.

Traders and investors

Many people think the terms *traders* and *investors* have virtually the same meaning, but actually they're quite different. A share trader usually buys or sells shares with the purpose of making a profit from the trades, so they don't hang on to shares for too long. In fact, a class of traders known as *day traders* aim to buy and sell the same shares on the same day so no positions are held overnight.

Generally traders make a profit by selling shares for more than they originally paid for them. Traders usually choose shares that are volatile — that is, their price rises and falls a lot in a relatively short period of time. These shares are the most risky and are usually shares issued by small businesses such as small mining companies or small biotechs and technology companies. These are also known as *speculative shares* or *speckies*.

Investors, on the other hand, buy shares and hold them for a reasonable period of time. If you're a share investor, you aim to put your spare cash to work to earn you a higher return than you could get from a bank account or similar type of investment. This is especially important in today's investing climate where interest rates are at a historical low. Investors usually purchase shares in larger businesses with a stable history of long-term profitability. These are also known as *blue chip* or *green chip* shares and they're inherently less risky.

Tip

Being successful as a full-time share trader is very difficult, so if you plan to give up your day job and become a professional share trader I suggest you think again. This book is written primarily for investors, so I won't really get into the finer aspects of trading shares for profit. Naturally, investors still need to be able to buy and sell shares and I explain how to do this in later chapters.

Making shares available for trading

As mentioned, if a company wants to go 'public' and issue shares that are then available to the general public, it needs to jump through a few hoops. The company is required to prepare a document called the *prospectus* that outlines the main features of the company and its proposed product (or products), as well as the financial details and risks involved for shareholders. A company going public is known as an *initial public offering* (IPO) or *float* because it's the first time the company is issuing shares that are available for the general public to purchase.

The main reason a company becomes a public one is that by doing so it can raise a substantial amount of capital. This capital is provided by people who participate in the float and purchase the shares. The capital the company receives this way is known as *equity capital*.

Comparing equity capital to loan capital

Another way a business can raise a substantial amount of capital is by means of business loans with a bank or other financial institution. This capital is naturally enough known as *loan capital*. Two different types of loans are possible:

- *Short-term loans:* Almost all businesses operate with a certain amount of credit. For example, if the business purchases goods, it's not usually on a cash on delivery (COD) basis. Instead, suppliers and contractors usually allow a one to two month delay before payment is required. The money the business owes in this way is an example of a short-term loan.

- *Long-term loans:* The amount of capital a business can obtain from short-term loans and the length of time the capital is available is limited. If a business needs a substantial amount of capital and wants this capital to be available for a longer period, it can apply to a bank or financial institution for a business loan. This is very similar to a mortgage, where interest is charged on the loan monthly but the loan is repaid over the longer term, which could be around 20 years.

For a business, equity capital has a big advantage over loan capital. Can you think what this is?

The answer is that equity capital is 'free', because the business isn't required to pay any interest on the capital and the capital doesn't need to be repaid.

It might surprise you to learn that from a shareholder's point of view it's usually better that the business has a reasonable amount of loan capital rather than trying to operate entirely on equity capital. The reason for this is that the business can usually use the loan capital to obtain a higher return on the capital invested than the cost of the interest on the loan. For example, if a business pays 6% interest on its long-term loan and can use this capital to generate a 10% profit, the business makes 4% clear profit on the loan capital and this benefits the shareholders.

Therefore, when a business has some loan capital, it doesn't need as much equity capital and so can have fewer shareholders — which, in turn, means that each shareholder benefits by getting a larger slice of the profit pie.

> ## Tip
>
> Although some loan capital is good, a business with too much loan capital is risky because it's vulnerable to downturns in business or the economy.

Becoming a shareholder

You can become a shareholder in a public company in two main ways: participating in a float or purchasing shares from someone else. I also cover some of the other, less common, ways of becoming a shareholder at the end of this section.

Participating in a float

To participate in a float (or IPO) you need to get a copy of the prospectus and provide the information required. You may do this using a paper copy of the prospectus or you might be able to do it electronically. In any case, you'll need to provide some financial information such as bank account details. You may also need to give some security details to ensure you're a bona-fide person and to prevent money laundering or tax evasion. Of course, you also have to pay for the shares you want. For example, if the issue price is $2.00 and you want 1000 shares, you'll have to cough up $2000. The float will have an expiry date and you need to make sure your application and application money are received before this date.

'I want to get these new shares before they're listed.'

Subscribing to a float and getting shares this way is similar to buying a new commodity such as a new car or book. The item hasn't had a previous owner and is unused so should be in perfect condition.

Purchasing shares from someone else

Once a company has floated and its shares are available through the securities exchange, you can buy shares in it from someone who wants to sell them, using the exchange trading facility. In past times, share trading was like an auction with buyers and sellers making deals directly, but nowadays it's done by a computer.

Now here's the catch: you can't deal directly with the exchange because to do so you need to be approved and licensed by them. So before you can trade shares, you need to find a licensed dealer who'll act on your behalf. These licensed dealers are known as *sharebrokers*, *stockbrokers* or simply *brokers*.

Naturally, brokers charge a fee for service that's known as *brokerage*, and this fee can vary a fair bit. Because many brokers offer their services, competition is fierce. This competition means lower prices so brokerage isn't a significant cost. Although you needn't worry too much about brokerage, but I do discuss it in more detail in chapter 7, when I explain how you can trade shares.

Buying shares through an exchange is similar to buying a second-hand commodity, such as a used car or used book. The shares have been pre-owned and aren't brand new.

Buying used shares and buying any other used commodity differs in one important way. Can you think what it is?

The answer is that with any physical commodity such as cars, books or clothing, the item has been previously used and is likely to show wear and tear. Also the item can become outdated or out of fashion because a new model comes on to the market. For example, with a motor car, the number of kilometres and its age are key factors in determining the car's value. With shares, the age of the shares or the number of previous owners doesn't matter at all because these factors have no influence on the share price. Shares aren't a physical commodity and don't age or become outdated. In fact, with quality shares the price is far more likely to rise with time than to fall.

Tip

I discuss the nuts and bolts of how you can trade shares in chapter 7.

Other ways of becoming a shareholder

You can become a shareholder in other ways than the two already mentioned. Some of these are:

- *Inheritance:* When a shareholder dies, the shares they own form part of their estate and will eventually be transferred to one or more of their beneficiaries. If you're one of those beneficiaries, the executors will arrange transfer of the shares into your name.

- *Private treaty:* As with any other commodity, transfer of share ownership can be arranged by direct negotiation between buyer and seller. In Australia, several thousand different shares are tradeable, not to mention the rest of the world, so it's generally not feasible to negotiate trades by private treaty (although some really large share transfers are negotiated this way).

- *Privatisation:* When the government decides to offload an asset, they usually do so by issuing shares. For example, Commonwealth Bank, Commonwealth Serum Laboratories, Qantas and Telstra were made available for public ownership in this way. Many Australians became shareholders by subscribing to the shares when they were first made available for purchase.

- *Structure change:* Many Australians became shareholders when mutual companies and friendly societies changed structure and became public companies. This was the case with many insurance companies and co-operative building societies.

- *Takeovers, mergers and splits:* Another way of becoming a shareholder in a listed company is through a takeover, merger or split. For example, the Bank of NSW was taken over by Westpac and the Sydney Futures Exchange merged with the ASX. In the opposite type of scenario, Coles Ltd became a listed company when Wesfarmers decided to get out of the grocery retailing business and make Coles a separate company (and no longer part of Wesfarmers).

Tip

Selling shares acquired in any one of the ways included in this section is likely to have tax implications, so you need to keep accurate records of the date and cost of the shares when you acquired them. I discuss this in greater detail in chapter 11.

Shares you can't buy

You might be surprised to learn that, despite the large number of different company shares traded on the Australian market, there are many, many more companies you can't buy shares in or subscribe to. This means you simply can't become a part-owner of the business, no matter how much you might want to. A large number of private companies (Pty Ltd) are held by private owners who want to retain the business and not transfer it to public ownership. A prime example is Aldi, which is a very successful and expanding supermarket chain in Australia. You can't become an Aldi shareholder because Aldi is a privately owned company and all profits flow back to the owners.

Another type of company you can't become a shareholder in directly is a fully-owned subsidiary company. A good example is Bunnings, which is a very successful hardware chain operating in Australia. You can't become a Bunnings shareholder because Bunnings is a fully-owned subsidiary of

Wesfarmers. The only way you can get a slice of the action at Bunnings is to buy Wesfarmers shares. The problem is that Wesfarmers owns a lot of other enterprises so when you buy Wesfarmers shares you get all the others in the package and Bunnings profits will be diluted.

Another problem is that many of the larger and most profitable companies that operate in Australia are based overseas and so their shares aren't listed with an Australian exchange. Examples of these include Google, Facebook, Microsoft and General Motors. In fact, the value of Australian listed shares is less than 2% of the world market. We are indeed small players!

Tip

Trading shares listed on overseas exchanges is possible if you deal with a broker who can arrange these types of trades. However, this introduces a raft of issues including currency exchange rates so I suggest that at this stage you stick to trading Australian listed shares.

Why share prices change

As you no doubt know, share prices change from day to day, or indeed during the course of one day's trading. The price fluctuates because of market forces. If more shares are wanted by buyers than are available from sellers, the price rises. If more shares are for sale than buyers for them, the price falls. It's really as simple as that. Shares are like any other traded commodity such as real estate or collectables. Short supply (where supply is less

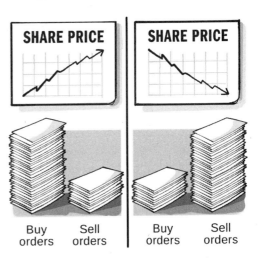

than demand) drives prices higher as buyers scramble to get in. Oversupply (supply greater than demand) drives prices lower as sellers scramble to get out. In the sharemarket, there's a constant interaction between buyers and sellers and this causes share prices to fluctuate.

Important share prices

There are several important share prices. These are fairly self-explanatory but I will outline them briefly here:

- *Opening price:* This is the price of the first trade for the day when the exchange opened.

- *High price:* This is the highest trade price for the day.

- *Low price:* This is the lowest trade price for the day.

- *Last price:* This is the price of the most recent trade.

- *Closing price:* This is the last price of the day (before the exchange closes).

- *Price change:* This is the amount by which the share price has changed. For example, after trading ceases for the day, the price change for the day is today's closing price minus yesterday's closing price. This could be zero if no price change occurred, or could be up (price rise) or down (price fall).

Within these prices, a heap of different scenarios are possible. Figure 2.1 shows just one scenario for a day's trading.

In this case, the shares closed yesterday at $1.50 and opened today at $1.45, before rising to a high of $1.60, falling to a low of $1.30 and then recovering to close the day at $1.40. This means the price change for the day was a fall of 10¢.

The scenario illustrated in figure 2.1 is a relatively complex one; often a share price moves in just one direction during the day's trading. For example, the price might rise or fall all day between opening and closing.

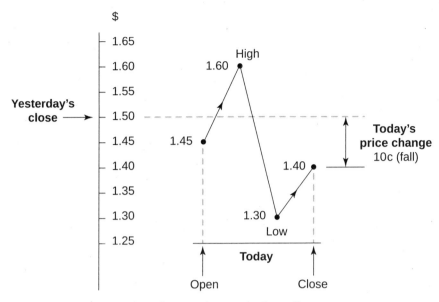

Figure 2.1: Possible price changes in one day's trading

After successive days, a price trend can become established. Analysis of trends is a very important aspect of share trading, and I discuss this in greater detail in chapter 9.

Tip

You might expect that today's opening price would be the same as yesterday's closing price but this isn't necessarily the case. When today's opening price isn't the same as yesterday's closing price (as in my example) this is known as a *gap*. In the hours between the closing trade one day and the following trading day's opening trade, a number of factors can affect a share price so gaps occur frequently.

Key takeaways

- Shares are units of ownership in a company and the number of shares you own determines the extent of your ownership. Shares are also known as *equities* and *stocks*.

- Shares are a financial security because they have a tradeable value.

- Shareholders are entitled to share in the assets and profits of the business they own shares in and to have a say in the running of the company. Shareholders can vote at AGMs (annual general meetings) and post questions.

- The main reason a business wants to go public and issue shares is so it can raise a substantial amount of money—known as *equity capital*.

- The other way a business can raise money is by loan capital—that is, by means of a business loan.

- The great advantage for a company of equity capital is that no interest or loan repayments are required.

- A shareholder can benefit if the business has some loan capital and can use it to make a higher profit than the interest cost of the loan. However, too much loan capital is undesirable.

- You can obtain shares by subscribing to the issue (float or IPO) when the shares are first made available to the public. You do this by completing the application form in the prospectus and submitting the required funds (based on the number of shares you want).

- The most common way of becoming a shareholder is to purchase shares in a company that's listed with an exchange.

- You can't deal directly with an exchange and need to become a client of a licensed broker who arranges trades on your behalf. The broker charges a fee—known as *brokerage*—which can vary widely between different types of broker.

- Some less common ways of becoming a shareholder include inheritance, privatisation of a government enterprise, demutualisation, takeover, merger or split, and private treaty (rare).

- Some profitable companies operating in Australia are privately owned so you can't become a shareholder in them.

- Share prices vary from day to day and indeed within a day according to supply and demand. More demand drives prices higher, whereas more supply drives prices lower.

- A share price can remain much the same or rise and fall continually during a day's trading.

- The price change for a share after trading ceases today is the difference between the closing price today and the closing price yesterday. It's possible for there to be no price change, a price rise or a price fall.

- If you have any queries related to your shareholding or dividends, you need to contact your broker or the appropriate share registry.

Chapter 3

Profiting from shares

The most likely reason you're reading this book and wanting to get into shares is because you hope (or expect) to make a profit by investing in them. You probably realise that any spare cash you have isn't earning much in the bank so you want to bring your money back from the holiday it's having and put it to work for you. And a great way of doing this is to invest in shares.

Despite all the different types of shares you can invest in and all the ins and outs of share investing, there are really only two ways you can profit from shares: capital gains and dividends. In this chapter, I outline both methods. I also explain the tax implications involved with share investing. You probably aren't really interested in taxation but it's important you understand the basics because they can affect your share investing decisions. I've tried to make this part as pain-free as possible.

Making profit from capital gains

I imagine that the idea of making profit from capital gains is already familiar to you. It's based on the principle that you buy something for a certain price and resell it later on for more than you paid for it. The difference is called a *capital gain* and it's the profit you make on the deal.

$$\text{Capital gain} = \text{net revenue} - \text{net cost}$$

Net revenue is the amount of money you receive from the sale minus any selling expenses. For example, if you invest in real estate, your net revenue is the selling price minus the expenses the agent charges for negotiating the sale.

Net cost is the money you had to shell out in the first place to buy, including any purchase expenses. With real estate, your purchase expenses include stuff such as solicitor's fees, government charges (including stamp duty) and the cost of searches or any building and pest inspections you want.

When you trade shares, your purchasing and selling expenses are small because they're usually only the brokerage involved in the buy and sell transactions (see figure 3.1). In some cases, bank charges may be incurred for money transfers but they're usually small unless overseas transfers are involved.

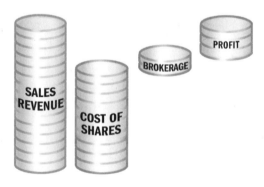

Figure 3.1: Brokerage is usually the only selling expense for shares

Capital gains profit with shares can be calculated using the following formula:

$$\text{Capital gain} = N \times (SP - CP) - E$$

Where
N = number of shares
SP = selling price of each share
CP = cost price of each share
E = expense involved with buying or selling (usually just the brokerage).

This formula will give you the correct answer for your capital gains profit unless the number of shares changes between the time you buy and the time you sell. If you buy and sell shares in different lots (or parcels), you need to calculate the capital gain with each parcel separately.

The formula I've just provided can look a bit intimidating if you're not mathematically inclined but it's really quite simple. All you're doing is calculating the profit on each share, and multiplying by the total number of shares to get your total profit. Then you're just subtracting your total expense.

Let's look at an example.

Say you buy 1500 shares for $4.20 and sell them later for $6.30. Brokerage is $15 on each transaction (the buy and the sell).

$$\begin{aligned}\text{Capital gain} &= 1500 \times (\$6.30 - \$4.20) - \$30 \\ &= 1500 \times \$2.10 - \$30 \\ &= \$3120\end{aligned}$$

That wasn't too hard was it?

Taxation and capital gains

Most people don't like to consider tax but unfortunately you may need to do so if you're required to submit a tax return. The tax rules applying to capital gains from share trading are basically the same as for any other commodity. Capital gains are considered income and need to be declared in the financial year of sale.

Here's the good bit: if you've held the shares for a year or more only half the capital gain counts as income. So in the preceding example, if you held the shares for less than a year the full $3120 would be taxable income, but if you held them for more than a year only half the profit ($1560) is taxable income.

Tip

Even if an accountant prepares your tax return, you need to be aware of the capital gains tax rules because they can affect your share investing decisions. For example, if you hold some shares for, say, 10 months or so, and you're thinking of selling them at a profit, it may well be a good idea to keep them until 12 months is up before you sell, so you can take advantage of the 50% profit discount.

Incurring a capital loss

Despite all your good intentions and research, some of your share trades will inevitably result in a loss. If the trade is a losing one, when you calculate your capital gain using the formula I gave you, you'll get a negative answer because you've sold the shares for less than what you paid for them (see figure 3.2).

Figure 3.2: Selling shares for less than you paid for them, results in a loss

The good news is that if you make a loss, you can write it off against your profit when working out your taxable income. For example, if you bought some shares and spent a total of $5000 on them but later sold them and recouped only $3000, you've incurred a loss of $2000. Let's say you made a profit of $4000 on some other trades. You can write the $2000 loss off against the $4000 profit and you need to declare only $2000 as taxable income.

That's the good news; the bad news is that capital losses can be written off only against capital gains and not against other taxable income. So if you've had a bad year with your shares and finish up at the end of the year with a net loss on your share trades, you can't write that loss off against your other taxable income for that year. All you can do is carry the loss forward to next year. There's no time limit and capital losses can be carried forward indefinitely.

Tip

If at the time of your death you're carrying forward a capital loss, that loss can't be used by your dependants. So if you know when you're going to die, it's a good idea to sell some of your profitable shares and write the loss of against your profits—otherwise, the loss will die with you. The only problem with this strategy is that you usually don't know when you're going to die!

Paper versus realised capital gains or losses

You can work out capital gains or losses based on the current prices of the shares you own compared to their cost when you bought them. These capital gains or losses are 'paper' gains or losses and not actual or realised gains or losses (because you haven't actually sold the shares).

For example, say you buy some shares and spend a total of $4000 on them. When you check prices, you're pleased to discover that the share price has risen and the shares are now worth $5000. Therefore, you're making a paper capital gain of $1000 on them. You decide (wisely) to hang on to the shares and not sell them. At the end of the year, you don't have to declare the profit in your tax return. Your profit is paper profit and not real profit and won't become real profit until such time as you sell. If you never sell, you don't have to declare any capital gains profits as income.

Tip

Everyone likes making a profit and no-one likes taking a loss—that's just human nature. Because you don't actually make a loss until you sell, this can result in a fear of loss (FOL) bias (discussed in chapter 5), which makes you tend to hang on to losers for longer than you should. The problem is that if you hold on to losers for too long, you're likely to end up making a greater loss than if you'd swallowed the bitter pill sooner and not procrastinated.

'I really should sell my XYZ shares … but
I have to overcome this hurdle.'

Tip

I discuss the important psychological factors that can affect your share trading decisions in later chapters.

Profiting from dividend income

The other way you can profit from shares is by receiving a dividend on them. If an Australian business makes a profit, it has to declare that profit and pay income tax according to Australian company taxation law. After the tax is paid the company can use the remaining profit in several ways:

- save it—that is, put the money into reserves and increase their capital pool

- reinvest it back into the business and upgrade machinery or equipment

- buy back their own shares that have previously been issued to reduce the number of shares in circulation

- buy (or take over) some other business

- reward executives and staff with salary increases or bonus payments

- reward shareholders by giving them a slice of the profit.

The way the after-tax profit pie will be divided up is decided by senior executives (board of directors) of the company. If they decide to pay a dividend, they also need to decide how much of the profit each share will receive. The amount allocated to each share is known as the *dividend per share* (DPS). If you're a shareholder, the total dividend payment you receive depends on how many shares you hold. Clearly, the greater the number of shares you hold, the greater your total dividend payment.

For example, say you hold 2000 shares in a company that pays a dividend of 25¢ per share. The total dividend you'll receive is:

$$2000 \times \$0.25 = \$500$$

If you'd held 1000 shares, your dividend would have been $250.

Issues relevant to dividends

You need to aware of a few issues relevant to dividends, discussed in the following sections.

Ex-dividend date

This is the cut-off date for receiving the current dividend. If you hold the shares before this date, you receive the current dividend (even if you sell the shares after this date). As you might expect, the share price invariably falls when the shares go ex-dividend and usually by the amount of the dividend per share, as shown in figure 3.3 (overleaf).

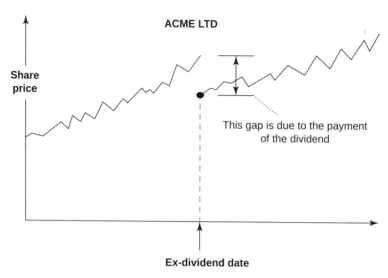

ACME LTD

Share price

This gap is due to the payment of the dividend

Ex-dividend date

Figure 3.3: The share price usually falls on the ex-dividend date

Tip

You won't receive the dividend on the ex-dividend date but at a later date—known as the *payment date* (and also the *allotment date* or *allocation date*). This date is usually a month or so after the shares go ex-dividend (as shown in figure 3.4).

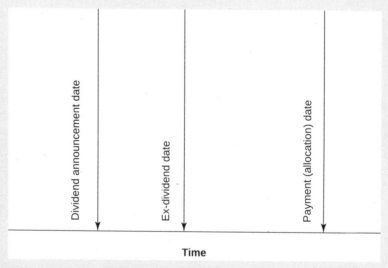

Dividend announcement date

Ex-dividend date

Payment (allocation) date

Time

Figure 3.4: The time delay between the ex-dividend date and the payment date.

Final and interim dividend

For most Australian companies, the year is divided into two six-month periods, and dividends are paid twice a year. The dividend for the first six months is called the *interim dividend,* and for the second is known as the *final dividend.* Often the final dividend is higher than the interim dividend, but not always, and sometimes they're the same. The total dividend is the sum of the two and is the dividend amount always quoted in financial reports.

Tip

If you find a share price has dropped suddenly overnight—that is, the shares open the next day at a lower price than they closed yesterday—check whether this gap was due to the shares going ex-dividend.

Dividend yield

The dividend yield (also known just as 'yield') is a very similar concept to interest on an account, because it's the percentage annual dividend return on the value of the shares. For example, if the yield is 4%, the dividend on those shares is providing a dividend return of 4% annually.

The yield is calculated by dividing the annual dividend per share in *cents* by the current share price in *dollars.*

Here's an example. Shares you own have an annual dividend of 45¢ per share and their share price is currently $9.62. Therefore, the yield on these shares is 45 ÷ 9.62 = 4.68%.

Effect of price changes

Even though the dividend paid usually changes only every six months, share prices change all the time, so the yield also changes with each change in share price. The yield moves opposite to the share price change, namely:

- If the share price rises, the yield falls.

- If the share price falls, the yield rises.

Tip

If you buy shares that pay a dividend, the yield would have been quoted at the time of purchase. Later on, as the share price changes, the yield also changes. You should always consider the current yield, not the yield at the time of purchase.

Dividend imputation and franking credits

Many investors find the dividend imputation and franking credits aspect of shares puzzling, but it's really not that hard. The best way to understand it is to go back in time before it existed. In those days, when some of the company's after-tax profit was used to pay shareholders a dividend, the total dividend received by each shareholder was regarded as income and taxed at the shareholder's income tax rate. This meant that the profit — which had already been taxed once — was taxed again. Of course, this was unfair, so the law was changed some time ago and nowadays when a shareholder receives a dividend, they're given credit for the tax already paid by the company. This credit is known as an *imputation credit* or *franking credit* and is paid to the shareholder by the ATO as a rebate on their taxable income. If the company pays full Australian tax on their profits, the dividend is fully franked (ff). In this case, if the shareholder is on a marginal tax rate of 30%, the dividend income they receive is effectively tax-free.

Now here's the really good part that applies to many retirees and people on pensions. If you don't pay income tax, you don't lose the imputation credits. The ATO still refunds the imputation credits as a nice, juicy cash payment! Sounds too good to be true? Well, it's true but has been a rather contentious issue. In the past, the Labor Party wanted to abolish dividend refund cash payments but this proved very unpopular with voters and was a major reason for their electoral defeat. But this change could be proposed again at some time in the future so you need to keep abreast of relevant developments.

If a company pays no Australian tax on their profits, the dividend is unfranked (uf) and a shareholder receives no imputation credits (or franking credits). In this case, the shareholder will need to pay full income tax on the dividend they receive at their marginal rate. Unfranked dividends occur if the company doesn't pay Australian tax on their profits. This can be for various reasons, of which the most likely is that the company is based overseas and doesn't have to comply with Australian tax law.

Level of franking

Different levels of franking are possible between unfranked (zero franking) and fully franked (maximum franking). Fortunately, you don't have to worry about calculating franking credits because when you receive your dividend statement from the share registry, it will clearly state the dollar value of any franking credits you're entitled to.

Comparing dividends with different franking levels

Franking credits are of great benefit to you whether or not you pay income tax. But how do you compare dividends when different levels of franking apply? For example, are you better off with shares that pay a 4% unfranked dividend or those with a 3% fully franked dividend?

You can work this out by using what's called the *grossing-up factor*. I won't go into the maths here but have provided table 3.1, which is an abbreviated table of grossing-up factors.

Table 3.1: Grossing-up factors for dividends with different franking levels

Franking level	Grossing-up factor
100%	1.43
50%	1.18
0	1.00

Tip

You can estimate the grossing-up factor for levels of franking in between those shown in table 3.1, but if you want to be really accurate please refer to one of my other books (for example, *Teach Yourself about Shares*, 3rd edition), where a full table of grossing-up factors is included.

Working out the true value of a yield

To get the true value of a yield, you just multiply the yield by the grossing-up factor to obtain a grossed-up yield. For example, a yield of 4% unfranked is still worth only 4% to you because the factor is 1.00. However, a yield of 3% fully franked is worth $3 \times 1.43 = 4.29\%$. Therefore, a 3% fully franked yield is better for you than a 4% unfranked one.

Another way of working this out is to apply your tax rate to the yield. For example, if your marginal tax rate is 30%, a 3% fully franked yield is still worth 3% after tax because with the franking credits the yield is effectively tax-free. But the 4% unfranked yield is worth only 4×0.7 for you after tax and so is only 2.8% net to you.

Tip

Get into the habit of considering the grossed-up yield of a share rather than the raw yield because the grossed-up yield is really the true value of the yield to you. Unfortunately, grossed-up yields aren't usually shown in the available statistics for shares so you need to work them out for yourself based on the level of franking.

Pitfalls of a high yield

Perhaps at first sight it seems that the higher the yield the better. Some shares may have a yield as high as 10%, which at first sight appears to be really great. But you need to consider that the yield may be high because the share price has fallen, and that's generally not a good sign. A high yield can also be an indication that the company is paying out too much of its profits and not re-investing enough back into the business. This makes it unlikely that the high dividend will continue in the future.

Tip

If a yield looks too good to be true, it probably is—and the shares could be shaky. This can be a trap you don't want to fall into so before you buy a high-yielding share, dig a little deeper and see if you can find the reason for the high yield. The best way of doing this is to look at the company's financial history. I show you how to do this in later chapters.

Considering dividend reinvestment plans

A dividend reinvestment plan (DRP) is a plan offered by some companies that allows you to take your dividend payment in additional shares rather than cash. Usually, the additional shares are offered at a discount price but this isn't always the case. When you become a shareholder in a company that has a DRP, you'll be given the choice of whether or not you want to join the plan. As far as the tax office is concerned, no difference is made between them and the same tax rules apply whether you take your dividend in cash or shares.

If you join the DRP, your dividend statement will show:

- the number of shares you held prior to the dividend
- the price of the shares allocated to you in lieu of cash
- the number of new shares you'll receive
- your total shareholding after you receive the new shares
- the value of the dividend in dollars
- the value of the imputation credits
- the allocation date for the new shares.

The allocation price multiplied by the number of shares is very unlikely to work out to be exactly the same as the dollar amount of the dividend, so you usually have some cash left over. This will be added to the amount of the next dividend and the carryover will be shown on your statement. If at some future time you sell all your shares, you'll receive the carryover amount in cash. In a few cases, the plan provides for rounding off the number of shares to the next highest number. In a few cases, the plan provides for rounding off the number of shares to the next lowest or highest number and no dollar carryover will be involved. If rounded down, you'll miss out on part of a share or if rounded up you'll receive it as an additional bonus.

Tip

You don't need to agonise whether or not to join a DRP when you first purchase a parcel of shares. You can change your mind at any time and you're not bound by your initial decision.

Let's look at a DRP example. Say the dividend on the number of shares you own is $536. The allocation price for the shares you receive under the plan is $8.20 per share. You also have $4.30 cash credit from the last dividend.

How many shares will you receive and what cash will be credited to you and carried over?

$$\text{Total cash available} = \$536 + \$4.30$$
$$= \$540.30$$
$$\text{Number of shares allocated} = \$540.30 \div \$8.20$$
$$= 65.89 \text{ shares}$$

So you'll receive 65 new shares and have the value of 0.89 of a share carried over.

The cash credited to your account and carried over to the next dividend will therefore be:

$$0.89 \times \$8.20 = \$7.30$$

Note: I've provided this example so you can understand how most DRPs work but you don't need to do any of the calculating provided here. It's all done for you and shown on your dividend statement.

Tip

If you don't need the dividend cash payment, I suggest you join the DRP. I explain why in chapter 12.

Comparing capital gains and dividends

The question of whether obtaining capital gains is better than getting dividends has been hotly debated for many years. Are you better off buying shares that offer the possibility of good capital gains or buying shares that have a reliable history of good dividend payments? At first sight, it might seem capital gains are the way to go. If the share price rises significantly you can sell the shares, cash in your profit and move on to the next trade. If you're able to do this several times a year, you'll end up with a handsome profit. If you hold the shares for longer than a year, only half the capital gain is taxable and that's also a better proposition than the 30% or so tax concession for fully-franked shares. These are sound arguments in favour of capital gains but the issue isn't actually that clear-cut. For a start, capital gains tax concessions can be obtained only if you own the shares for a year or more and, further, they can be declared only once—when the shares are sold. On the other hand, if you hold shares over the long term, the dividend franking credits go on year after year.

Another problem with capital gains is that to make good profits from them, you need shares that are of the more volatile kind and so inherently more risky. In contrast, companies that have a history of good dividend payments over a number of years are likely to be far more stable. They seldom change their dividend policy (unless some severe event causes a large drop in profits, such as occurred during the COVID-19 pandemic). So the question really resolves itself according to the time frame of your investment. If you're into shares for the longer term—that is, you're an investor rather than a trader—good dividends are well worthwhile, especially if the dividend has a high level of franking. On the other hand, if you're more a trader than an investor and want fast profits in the short term, capital gains are the way to go.

Tip

The ideal situation is to get both benefits with your shares—that is, you receive a steady dividend over the years and the shares also rise in value. These are the types of quality shares I suggest you consider for your core portfolio. By all means, you can also have some speculative shares that offer the possibility of high capital gains as satellites to your core.

The importance of return on capital

Many people think that dollar profit is the most important consideration with any investment. For example, if a friend tells you that their profit from share investing was $10 000, what would your reaction be? Would you pat your friend on the back and say 'well done', or would you think it wasn't much good at all?

'I've been going okay with my shares. I'm making $10 000 in profit!'

The answer is that you can't actually tell how good the profit was because two vital pieces of info are missing. Can you think what they are?

The two vital bits of info missing are the amount of money your friend invested in shares and the time period over which the profit was made. This info allows you to work out the *return on capital invested*, and this figure is more significant than straight profit.

For example, if your friend invested $50 000 in shares and made a $10 000 profit in a one-year period, that would be great because their return on investment would be 20%. If the sum invested was $100 000, that would still be good but not as great because the return on investment is now 10%. If they invested $250 000 in shares, their return on investment wouldn't be much good at all because it's only 4%. The time period for the investment is also important. If the profit had been made on $250 000 over a two-year period, their profit would be rather paltry—only a 2% pa (per year) return on capital invested.

So you can see that the real measure of profitability is the return on capital invested expressed as a percentage pa. You can calculate it using the following formula:

$$\text{ROC} = \left(\text{yearly profit / capital invested}\right) \times 100$$

Note: You convert the decimal to a percentage by multiplying by 100.

If the time period isn't one year you can work out an equivalent return on capital for one year by multiplying by the following factor:

$$12 \div \text{number of months}$$

For example, if the time period is six months the factor is 2 (12 ÷ 6), but if the time period is two years the factor is 0.5 (12 ÷ 24).

Tip

The same principles apply to companies: knowing how much profit a company made in dollars is really quite meaningless. You need to know how much capital was invested in their business and the time period over which the profit was made. (For more discussion of this, see chapter 8.)

Key takeaways

- You can profit from shares in two ways—capital gains and dividends.

- You make a capital gain if you sell shares for more than what you paid for them.

- Dividends are very similar to interest on an account, and the more shares you hold, the greater your dividend payment.

- The statistic that tells you how much dividend bang you'll get for your investment buck is the yield. As with interest, yield is a percentage and is calculated by dividing the total annual dividend (in cents) by the share price (in dollars).

- Dividends can be fully franked (ff), partly franked (pf) or unfranked (uf). The higher the franking, the better—because the tax office refunds the franking credits you're entitled to.

- Payment of the next dividend has a cut-off date, known as the *ex-dividend date*. If you hold the shares (or buy them) before this date, you'll get the next dividend; if you sell them before this date, you lose out.

- On the ex-dividend date, the share price falls usually by the amount of the dividend.

- The yield rises and falls in the opposite way to the share price. That is, a rising share price results in a lower yield and a falling price results in a higher yield.

(continued)

- The true value of a dividend depends on the grossed-up yield. To obtain it, multiply the raw yield by the grossing-up factor, which varies with the level of franking.

- Some companies that pay a dividend give you the option of taking the dividend payment in shares by offering a dividend reinvestment plan (DRP). If you don't actually need the cash, I suggest you join the plan. I explain my reasoning in chapter 12.

- High capital gains are more likely with speculative shares. You don't want to hold on to these types of shares for too long but they can be satellites in your portfolio. If you're a longer term investor, the ideal situation is to make both capital gains and dividends from your core shares.

Chapter 4

Is share investing gambling?

I'm often asked the following question: is share investing any different from gambling? I suspect many would-be share investors think that share investing is really just a more sophisticated form of gambling. Consequently, if they don't like gambling, they shy away from shares. This is a shame because, as I show you in this chapter, despite the similarities there are some significant differences. These differences are very important and you shouldn't be deterred from share investing because you really aren't a gambler. I've never been a gambler, and would be lucky to place a bet once a year; yet, I've been a share investor for over 50 years.

The question is also more profound than it would seem at first sight. In answering it through this chapter, I uncover some fundamental issues of importance. First let's consider the similarities before considering the differences.

Similarities between share investing and gambling

Share investing and gambling have four basic similarities—namely:

1. Success or failure involves a future outcome.

2. An element of risk is involved.

3. A sum of money is at stake.

4. Another party has taken the opposite view.

Success or failure involves a future outcome

'What's the future for these shares?'

When you gamble, you base your bet on the outcome of a future event. For example, in the game of two-up you try to predict whether tossed coins will come down odds or evens. In a sporting contest, you try to predict which team will win and, in a horse race, which horse will cross the finish post first. With share investing, you try to predict how a particular company's shares will perform in the future. Will they rise or fall? Will the company increase or decrease profitability? Will some new venture be successful or not?

An element of risk is involved

Both share investing and gambling involve risk. This is another way of saying the outcome isn't certain and this, in turn, means there's the possibility of winning or losing. If your prediction turns out to be correct, you win and make a profit; if you're wrong, you lose and incur a loss.

The notion of future unpredictability is a basic principle of chaos theory, with a major reason being that you can never know the initial conditions exactly. And if you don't know the initial conditions precisely, predicting a future outcome with certainty is impossible. Prior to a race commencing, punters don't know precisely the condition of each horse and jockey and the track at the time. Meteorologists don't know the precise weather conditions in every part of the planet and share investors don't know the precise details about everything going on in a company or its competition, which can affect the performance of its shares. Therefore, no highly experienced share investment advisor or clever super-duper computer program can make correct predictions all the time about the sharemarket or any particular share.

Tip

I introduced you to the principle of uncertainty with shares in chapter 1. Head back to this chapter if you need a refresher.

A sum of money is at stake

Gamblers and investors have some cash they're prepared to stake on the outcome of a future event. They do so in the hope (or expectation) of making a profit—that is, to increase the initial stake.

Another party has taken the opposite view

A gambler can't place a bet unless another party is prepared to take the opposite view and 'cover' the bet. For a sporting event, the other party could be the TAB or other betting institution; for a game of two-up, another gambler is prepared to bet 'odds' if you bet 'evens'; and, in a game of poker, the house or another gambler covers the bet. With shares, the other party is an investor or financial institution prepared to sell when you want to buy or buy when you want to sell.

Tip

It's worth remembering that when you trade shares, you can't buy unless someone else is prepared to sell and you can't sell unless someone else is prepared to buy. Therefore, you can't be certain that the trade will always work in your favour—it may turn out that the other party was correct and not you.

'Is now the time to sell them ... or to buy them?'

Differences between share investing and gambling

So far I've pointed out the similarities between share investing and gambling. Now is the time to consider the differences. They are:

- Shares allow you to limit your loss.

- Shares allow you to vary the risk.

- Shares and gambling have different time frames.

- Shares have more useful information available.

- Shares allow you to manage your decisions.

- Everyone can be a winner with shares.

Shares allow you to limit your loss

With gambling, if you lose you generally lose your entire stake, whereas with shares, this is unlikely and shouldn't occur except on very rare occasions. If you buy shares that fall in price, you certainly lose some of the money you've invested. You could lose all of your invested money if you hold shares in a company that becomes bankrupt and the shares cease trading and so become valueless. This seldom happens and only then with very speculative and risky shares. The chance of quality types of Australian companies suddenly changing from prosperous ones to going out of business is almost zero.

In any case, if an established business starts to fall on hard times, you'll be given plenty of warning signs and, if you heed these, you can bail out. You will incur some loss but certainly shouldn't lose all of your invested capital.

> ## Tip
>
> With shares you've purchased, you can place a *limiting loss order*, so that whatever happens you don't lose more than a certain amount—say, 10% or 20%. You can't do this with a gambling bet. I discuss limiting loss type orders in chapter 10.

Shares allow you to vary the risk

With gambling, you generally can't vary the risk. It's true that for events such as horse racing, different horses have different odds quoted and you can decide if you'll bet on a favourite or an outsider. But with most forms of gambling, you can't vary the odds—for example, this is the case with a poker machine or the toss of a coin or a lottery.

On the other hand, with shares you can always vary the risk. If you want to take a low risk, you can invest in

'I can't ever see this happening!'

shares issued by an established and prosperous company. I call these types of shares *quality* ones. If you want to take more risk, you can purchase some speculative shares (or *speckies*) in the hope of a quick capital gain. These types of shares are usually low in price and, therefore, you can make a much greater profit on your capital invested with a small rise in price.

The following example demonstrates this. Say the price of a share rises by 10¢. What's your percentage profit if the purchase price of the share was (a) 10¢ or (b) $2.00?

(a) Your percentage profit is $10 \div 10 = 1 = 100\%$. (You've doubled your money.)

(b) Your percentage profit is $10 \div 200 = 0.05 = 5\%$. (Not nearly as flash is it?)

Shares and gambling have different time frames

With gambling, the time frame is usually short—maybe only a few seconds to an hour or so. It doesn't take long to roll dice or throw coins or for a race or sporting event to finish. This is a large part of the attraction of gambling and why it can become addictive—because the buzz of winning occurs with little delay or can result in virtually instant gratification.

On the other hand, share investing is generally a longer term proposition that can vary from a few days to months or years. In fact, many of the shares in my portfolio are ones I purchased 20 or more years ago.

It's true that some share trades can be of relatively short duration. Some professional share traders—known as *day traders*—buy and sell the same shares during a single day. But you're unlikely to do this and you'll generally invest over the longer term. I recommend that share investing for you should definitely be a longer term proposition for most of your capital, and not a quick way of trying to get rich.

Tip

It's important to realise that with shares you seldom get quick gratification. You need a fair amount of patience if you're to be a successful share investor.

Shares have more useful information available

Most gambling decisions can be described as 'impulsive' or 'spur of the moment' and don't involve much information analysis. For example, you don't need to analyse information to decide if you'll bet 'heads' or 'tails' on the toss of a coin or which poker machine to play. It's true that with some forms of gambling information may be available that the gambler can analyse before the bet is placed. For example, with a horse race a gambler may access a form guide and know how each horse and jockey has performed in the past. The same applies to a team contest. However, with racing or team events, the result on the day will usually depend primarily on conditions at the time rather than on past performance. This type of knowledge is inaccessible to the gambler unless they're able to access some 'insider knowledge' that's not available to all.

Tip

In events where the outcome is purely random, such as the toss of a coin, some gamblers analyse successive outcomes and use false reasoning known as the *gambler's fallacy*. This is based on the notion that if a similar outcome has occurred for a prolonged period, the opposite outcome is now more likely. For example, if 10 heads in a row are thrown, almost all gamblers would bet on tails on the next throw, believing it to be the more likely outcome. This is false reasoning and contradicts the basic premise that the outcome of each event is random.

Unlike gambling, with share investing a large amount of reliable information is usually accessible—especially about companies that have been in business for a long time. To be a successful share investor, your decisions should be considered ones and not the 'spur of the moment' type. You can readily access the information you need to make an informed decision.

Tip

In later chapters, I show you how to access the information you need about shares. It's downright foolish not to avail yourself of it.

Shares allow you to manage your decisions

When you gamble, you place your bet and hand over your stake—and in the vast majority of cases that's the end of it until the coins are tossed, the dice is rolled, the button is pressed, the race is run or the lottery is drawn. After you place your bet, you can usually do no more to change any aspect of it, and you simply have to watch and wait until the event takes place, and then find out whether your bet has been a profitable one. (Although some online gambling overseas does allow live or 'in-play' betting.)

With shares, the longer time frame allows you to manage your investment and make adjustments as time goes on. If you've purchased a share that rises in price, you can think about buying some more or else sell and cash in your profit. Conversely, if the price falls, you can sell the shares and limit your loss, or buy the share back later if the price rises again. You can't do this with gambling—you simply can't modify your bet as time goes on regardless of the unfolding outcome.

'I'll see how my shares perform and then I'll decide.'

You can imagine shares as similar to a continual race with shares running around a racetrack with no winning post—so the race has no end. You can watch the race and see how your share is performing, and then decide at any time whether you want to take some action. For example, if your share is flagging and falling behind, you can cash in your investment and take a loss; if your share is up with the leaders and doing well, you can hold on to it and maybe increase your stake. This is part of the process of managing your investment that's so important with shares.

Everyone can be a winner with shares

With gambling, there are winners and losers. This follows from the very nature of gambling. For example, if six players sit down for a night of poker, some will finish the night as winners, and some as losers. This is because the game is a *zero-sum game,* which simply means that the sum of the winnings must equal the sum of the losses. For example, if one player finishes the night with a win of $100, one or more other players must have lost a total of $100. But shares aren't necessarily a zero-sum game and so share investing is very different. If the sharemarket rises, all investors can potentially benefit from the rise and be winners. This is possible because when the market rises, the total money pool invested in shares increases.

Naturally, the opposite scenario applies; if the market as a whole drops, potentially all share investors can lose. These scenarios are described by the saying, 'When the tide rises all boats lift, and when the tide falls all boats drop'.

With shares, this saying doesn't usually apply for every share because it's very rare for all shares to move in the same direction at the same time. In other words, when the market as a whole rises, it's very unusual for all shares to rise in price and, similarly, when the market falls, some shares will usually buck the trend and rise. It's also possible that some shares don't move much despite market rises or falls. However, it's safe to say that when the market rises or falls, the majority of shares tend to move with the market.

'You see, all boats rise on a rising tide.'

As I pointed out earlier in this chapter, if you buy shares someone else must sell, and if you sell someone else must buy. If shares rise in price after a trade, the buyer wins but the seller loses. The seller would have made more profit by hanging on to the shares and selling them later at a higher price. However, the seller in this scenario can still be a winner if the proceeds from the sale of those shares are used to buy other shares that later rise in price. So, unlike gambling, every share investor can be a winner—especially when the market rises. Remarkably with shares, a very simple strategy can enable you to make a profit even when the market is flat or is falling a bit. Intrigued? I explain the strategy in chapter 12 but until you get there, it's important to bear in mind that this strategy depends on good money management.

Key takeaways

- Share investing and gambling have some similarities, but also some significant differences.

- One of the main differences is that with shares you can limit your loss to a certain percentage of your outlay. You certainly can't do this with a gambling bet.

- Another difference is that share investing involves a longer time frame. Share traders often work with short time frames but you should regard yourself as an investor rather than a trader.

- Another difference with shares is that you can obtain heaps of info and this is usually not available with most forms of gambling. Even if gambling info is available, it usually doesn't help much because the result on the day usually depends as much on the latest conditions as past results. And the most important conditions at the time will usually be unknown.

- Another difference is that with shares you can manage them as time goes on. For example, if you buy a share that turns out to be a winner, you can buy some more or cash in your profits. With gambling, you can't do this. In the vast majority of cases, you can't cash in or change your bet halfway through a horse race or team contest.

- You can imagine share investing as being similar to a race with shares running around a track that has no winning post. The race continues indefinitely and you can opt in or out or change your bet at any time you choose.

- Another huge difference is that share investing doesn't necessarily result in winners and losers. If the market rises, everyone with shares can be a winner and participate in the rise. In gambling, another party has to cover the bet by taking the opposite view so it's impossible for both parties involved in the bet to win.

Chapter 5

Benefits
and pitfalls
of share investing

In this chapter, I consider how profitable shares have been as an investment for Australians. I discuss the benefits of investing in shares along with the possible pitfalls, and also outline some principles you can apply to improve your share profits. These principles are so important I have called them *Golden Rules*. I strongly urge you to come to terms with these rules and apply them to your shares transactions.

When I look back over my many years of share investing, I won't profess that all of my investments were good ones. In fact, I have to confess that I've had quite a few disasters. When I've subsequently analysed what went wrong with these investments, I've realised that in almost all instances the loss was the result of not sticking to my own rules. I acted on the advice or recommendations of others, for example, and short-circuited my usual rules and procedures. This is why I urge you to follow the rules outlined in this chapter, rather than acting in an impulsive manner or blindly taking the advice of others—no matter how good their reputation may be.

Are shares a good investment?

What is the best longer term investment for Australians? It's a question that continually surfaces for discussion. The main contenders for 'best investment' are shares, property, bonds, fixed interest, superannuation or mortgage payments. More recently, overseas shares have been thrown into the mix because investing in international shares is now a feasible proposition for Australians.

This question has no definite answer because the best investment for you may not be the best investment for someone else. You have your own, unique conditions and investment expectations. Some factors to consider are:

- *Your age and stage of life:* For example, a young person embarking on their working career is likely to have completely different investment expectations than a settled middle aged person with older children, or a retiree.

- *Your financial situation:* You could be in the early stages of settling down and desperately trying to save every spare penny and build up enough cash for a deposit on your first home. You could be middle aged and well off with a high disposable income. You could be retired with a nest egg you've accumulated over the years or from superannuation you've cashed in. Or you could be a pensioner with limited funds to invest.

- *Your financial priorities:* These priorities stem naturally from your financial situation; younger people are usually trying to build their wealth as rapidly as possible whereas older people are usually more interested in conserving what they already have.

- *Your gender:* Males and females usually have a different outlook on investing. Males (especially younger males) tend to be more daring and take more risks and trade more often, whereas females are usually more conservative, trade less and are more risk averse. The more conservative approach usually turns out to be the best one over the longer term and, for this reason, women tend to be more successful share investors than men.

Performance of Australian shares

How have shares performed as an investment for Australians? I won't consider directly investing in international shares because they introduce a whole heap of complicating factors and are really not suitable for beginner share investors. The short answer is that some Australian shares have performed very well over the years and had you invested in them some time ago you would be very rich now. Examples that spring to mind are Commonwealth Bank and CSL, just to name two. (The issue price for Commonwealth Bank shares at their IPO in 1991 was $5.40. They're now trading at around $100 per share.)

On the other hand, some Australian shares have been 'dogs' and haven't rewarded investors at all. Instead, they have been losing propositions. For example, investing in one of the market 'darlings' AMP in March 2018 would have brought you only pain as the shares dived from $5.00 to $1.20—a fall of 76%—in the space of two years!

Suppose you had a diversified portfolio of different Australian shares in different sectors of the market. How would you have fared over the years? Or more to the point, how can you expect your capital to build in the future compared to other types of investment? Well, the simple answer is that shares and property have consistently been the two best investments for Australians over the longer term.

Beyond the sheer profit number crunching, however, you have many other factors to consider with an investment. Property doesn't suit many investors because it usually involves considerable hassles and maintenance, and is certainly not a buy and forget proposition. You also need a heap of saved capital before you can put your foot on the bottom rung—you can hardly go to your bank with savings of a few thousand dollars and expect the bank to lend you several hundred thousand dollars. And you can hardly go to a real estate agent with a few thousand dollars in your kitty and expect to be shown some suitable real estate—you wouldn't even get to see a block of land in a remote area. Even if you could find some financial institution prepared to lend you heaps of money, would you really want to saddle yourself with huge loan repayments for a long time into the future?

If you don't have enough savings to put down a sizeable deposit on a property or you simply don't want the hassles that could be involved, where can you invest your spare cash? After the financial scare caused by COVID-19 in 2020, the answer for many Australians was to put their spare cash into a home loan or superannuation account, or simply deposit it in a savings account with a financial institution. Putting spare money into a home loan reduces the debt and the minimum loan repayments and is a basically a good idea if you have a suitable loan that allows you to vary your repayments. But if you don't have a long-term loan, you obviously can't do this. Putting money into superannuation enables you to obtain good government tax concessions and increase your retirement payout. The downside is that your money is locked away — meaning you can't normally access the benefit of the increased payout until you retire. If you're not close to retirement age, that could be many years into the future. Cash deposits or term loans aren't really a good idea when interest rates are low. That's certainly the case at the time of writing and is likely to remain so for the foreseeable future. In fact, interest rates are so low that any interest paid probably won't even keep up with inflation. This means that your real wealth (in terms of the purchasing power of your money) will actually decrease.

Even if you can pay down a long-term debt, it may not be such a good idea if the interest rate on the loan is less than you could earn on your money by investing elsewhere. Naturally, because this book is about shares, the specific elsewhere I'm thinking about is shares.

Here's an example of the benefits of investing in shares rather than paying down a loan more quickly. Nowadays, a typical interest rate on a home loan is about 3%. This means that if you use your savings to pay down the loan more quickly, the money you repay is actually earning you 3%. So the comparison really boils down to this: can you expect to consistently earn more than 3% (after tax) on a relatively safe share investment? If you can do so, you're better off investing any spare funds you have into shares rather than paying down your home loan. I'm confident you'll be able to earn more than 3% on a share investment — provided you adhere to the rules and adopt the strategies I explain in this chapter (and later on in the book).

A great beauty of shares is that you don't need a lot of money to start investing. The other great feature is that getting into or out of shares involves very little hassle, and virtually no hassle is involved in holding them. To get into shares, all you need to do is establish an account with a broker and away you go! Actually, I'll qualify that—you do need a certain amount of basic knowledge to improve your chances of success and to avoid disasters.

> **Tip**
>
> Hold off on plunging into investing in shares until you've read this book in its entirety.

Riskiness of shares

As everyone knows, shares are a more risky form of investment than a term loan or bank deposit. There's no way round this because of the relationship between risk and return (covered in chapter 1). So if you want a higher return, you need to be prepared to take more risk. However, shares are often regarded as a more risky proposition than they actually are. One reason for this is that share prices are widely reported on a daily basis in media such as the radio and TV news. This emphasises the short-term price fluctuations rather than the long-term trends, and gives the impression that shares are risky. With other investments such as property, the owner doesn't get a day-to-day valuation and simply has no idea about short-term value fluctuations.

Many investors (or would-be investors) get spooked with shares when the market takes a sudden large dive—as occurred in early 2020 as the COVID-19 pandemic took hold throughout the world. During the early stages of the pandemic, many share investors panicked, took flight and sold most (if not all) of their shares. Was this a good strategy? Well, no, because before long the shares started to recover and, by mid-2021, had regained all of the value lost due to the pandemic. Indeed, soon the sharemarket reached higher levels than those before the pandemic.

Figure 5.1 (overleaf) shows the sudden fall in the Australian All Ordinaries index (which tracks the 500 largest companies listed on the Australian Securities Exchange), and its recovery through 2020.

Clearly, if you picked out the short period from just after the pandemic took hold until the time when the sharemarket bottomed, you'd come to the conclusion that shares weren't a good investment at all. As shown in figure 5.1, the Australian market (as measured by the All Ords index) fell from 7200 to 4600 in the space of just one month. During this period, you'd have been much better off leaving your money in the bank or investing in fixed-interest type securities where your savings would have been protected from the falls.

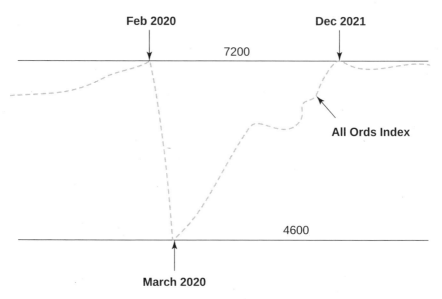

Figure 5.1: Fall and rise of the All Ordinaries index in 2020

In the last 20 years or so, similar scenarios have unfolded — which just goes to show that history has a way of repeating itself. For example, the sharemarket experienced similar huge hits after the terrorist attacks in New York in 2001 and during the GFC (global financial crisis) of 2007–08. During both periods, the sharemarket dived like a stone; however, the market recovered some time later and carried on regardless.

Time period of share investing

Share investing should be regarded as a longer term proposition. If you'd taken a longer term view and not panicked when these events took place, you'd have simply hung on to your share portfolio. It's very tempting to think you could have sold when the market first dived and later bought back when the market recovered, and made a motza. This seems to be a really good strategy but, in practice, applying it is not at all straightforward.

Picking the top and bottom of the market in real time is notoriously difficult, and it could well be that by the time you decide to sell your shares, the price could have already fallen a great deal. When you decide it's time to buy back in, the market could already have risen a lot and you might end up having to buy back the shares you sold at a higher price than they were when you sold them! Another consideration is that if you sell all your shares in one year, you'll most likely incur a big capital gains tax bill for that year and end up giving much of your profit to the tax office.

Tip

Over the longer term, despite the ups and downs, Australian shares have proven to be a much better investment than safer options such as bank deposits or fixed-interest investments. As a share investor, you should look at longer term trends rather than short-term choppiness.

Positives of share investing

Shares have many great features that make them well worthwhile as an investment if you have some spare cash—and you want to put that cash to work and not leave it sunbaking on the seaside.

The positives of share investing include:

- *High rate of return:* Good quality shares consistently produce high returns over the longer term.

- *Liquidity:* You can buy and sell most shares very quickly and easily—a feature known as *liquidity*. Share trades are now settled within two business days, which means you can convert most shares into cash or cash into shares in just two days. (See the next chapter for more on liquidity.)

'Up you get! I've got work for you.'

- *Ease of trading:* Share trading is easy and hassle-free. After you've established an account with a broker, you can trade shares from the comfort and convenience of your own home or even when you're out and about if you have a suitable mobile device.

- *Low trading cost:* The trading cost of share transactions is really peanuts. For example, you can trade $10000 worth of shares online for as little as $20, and with some online brokers trading can be even cheaper.

- *No holding costs or hassles:* You can hold millions of dollars' worth of shares for years, and doing so will cost you absolutely nothing. When you own shares, any capital gains and dividends you receive come at no extra cost to you. You can't get a better deal than that!

- *Diversity:* With shares you can spread your wings widely — you're not committed to just one type of enterprise. You can invest in as many different types of businesses as you want.

- *Flexibility:* You can vary the investment amount to suit your needs. You could invest as little as $500 in speculative shares and at the same time invest $10000 in quality ones.

- *Taxation benefits:* As covered in chapter 3, if you invest in shares that pay a franked dividend, the franking credits are returned to you. Depending on the level of franking, the dividend can actually be tax-free. Even better, if you don't pay income tax, the franking credits are paid to you as cash. If you sell shares you've held for a year or more, only half the profit is taxable. If you've made a loss, you can carry it over and write it off against future profits.

Investing rules

To improve your investing success with shares, I now outline the important Golden Rules I suggest you adopt.

Golden Rule 1: Use rational decision-making

My first rule is to try to base your share decisions on evidence and rational considerations rather than emotions or instincts.

That is, you should try to be dispassionate and keep your emotions in check when you make decisions about shares. Try to avoid panic should the market as a whole or a particular share tumble. At the other end of the spectrum, try not to get 'hyped up' and carried away with undue optimism when the market or a particular share price is rising steeply.

I know this is easy to say but difficult to apply. The real danger with instincts and emotions, however, is that they tend to cause you to act in certain ways without even realising why you're doing so. If you're aware of them, hopefully you can be more in charge of them, and you'll not let emotions and instincts unduly influence your share decisions. To help you to do this, the following sections outline three common emotions and instincts that can bias your sharemarket decisions. These are:

- fear of missing out (FOMO)

- fear of loss (FOL)

- confirmation bias.

Fear of missing out

The fear of missing out (FOMO) is a very common emotion with investors (and people generally). Naturally, seeing others making a motza when you're not is very disconcerting. So your natural instinct is to try to get on board and join the party. The FOMO instinct generally shows up as a desire to purchase shares you don't already own.

'I'd better get on board. I don't want to miss out.'

Tip

In chapter 10, I outline plans that apply to share trading. Before hitting the buy button on any share investment, I suggest you pause, take some time out, perhaps make yourself a tea or coffee, and ask yourself, 'Does this purchase conform to my plan?' This may help you to realise your desire to buy the shares could be primarily based on the FOMO instinct.

Here is a good example of the FOMO mentality that shows how disastrous it can be.

In early 2021, Elon Musk, the world's richest man, advised his Twitter followers (of which there were millions) to change their allegiance from WhatsApp Messenger to an encrypted messaging app such as Signal. Unfortunately, many of Musk's faithful followers rushed out and bought shares in a listed company with this name. However, the listed company they purchased was a small medical concern and not in the business of messaging. The shares in this company soon rose over 11000% in three days—rising from about US $0.60 to over $70! After a few days, the mistake was uncovered and panic selling took hold as investors who had bought in tried to get out again. Needless to say, the price of Signal shares dived as quickly as they had risen, and those foolish enough to buy at elevated prices suffered huge losses.

Clearly those who bought the shares in Signal had followed a 'shoot now, ask questions later' approach. The FOMO instinct drove them to buy shares without really understanding what they were getting into. Certainly, these investors can't have done even the most basic research before plunging in—namely, to find out what type of company they were buying shares in, what its products were and whether the company was profitable (or could be expected to be in the future).

Tip

Remember this example of Signal shares should you feel tempted to rush out and buy shares because you don't want to miss out on what you think might be a good thing when you haven't researched those shares to understand what you could be getting into.

Fear of loss

No doubt you like to win and don't like to lose. Psychological experiments have proven that the fear of loss (FOL) is actually a more powerful instinct than the desire to win. With shares, you don't actually make a real loss until you sell, so FOL shows itself as a reluctance to sell. As long as you don't sell shares, your loss is just a 'paper loss' and not a real one. So your natural instinct will likely be to want to keep holding on to losing shares, hoping the losers will stage a turnaround and become winners. It's my experience that this seldom happens—at least in the shorter term. Often, the longer you hang on, the more you lose.

Another reason for the FOL instinct is that if you sell and take a loss you're really admitting you made a mistake. After all, you bought the shares in the first place because you thought they would be winners. If they instead turn out to be losers, you have to admit you were wrong. We all get a buzz telling anyone who wants to listen how much profit we made with shares, but we really don't like confessing (even to ourselves) when we are wrong!

'FOMO, I don't want to miss out. But FOL, I don't want to lose!'

The FOL instinct tends to act in opposition to FOMO, so a constant tug of war takes place between them in your mind. The winner often depends on your general mood. If you feel optimistic, FOMO tends to overcome FOL; when you're feeling pessimistic, FOL tends to gain the upper hand.

Tip

You can always sell a losing share before you've incurred a big loss with it. If you do sell, you can still keep an eye on the share and buy it back if conditions change and the share starts to look good again.

Confirmation bias

As we go through life, we develop a belief system on things that affect us. Because we're all different, we all have our own beliefs—that's partly what makes each of us a unique human. Once we've developed our core belief system, we tend to take on board any evidence that confirms our existing beliefs and, in doing so, our beliefs are reinforced. At the same time, we tend to ignore any evidence that contradicts our beliefs, because we don't want to be wrong. We justify this bias in many ways—such as by regarding contradictory evidence as being irrelevant.

'I think I'll only read this one.'

As you get into shares, you'll no doubt find that you favour some shares or types of shares rather than others. Also, as you develop, you'll most likely start to access more information. This is when confirmation bias can rear its ugly head. For example, if you've bought some shares based on information that led you to believe they could be winners, you tend to only take on board any evidence that reinforces this belief, ignoring any that contradicts it. This can cause you to hang on to losers or miss out on buying new shares that could be winners. Instead, you can get into a rut that is difficult to climb out of.

Tip

To overcome confirmation bias, you need to try to be rational and not let ingrained biases affect your decisions. Instead, try to judge new information on its merits and in a fair manner.

Golden Rule 2: Limit your losses but let your profits run

I'll hang on!

WINNING SHARE

If you're on to a winner, hang on to it and ride your winner for as long as your profit continues. On the other hand, if you're on to a loser, don't continue to hang on. Get out, sell your loser and limit your loss. In years gone, a well-known advertisement for a popular flyspray showed a fly on the tail of a running dog with the caption, 'When you're on to a good thing, stick to it'. This metaphor can also be applied to share investing—when the running dog is a winning share.

> **Tip**
>
> Try to remember this metaphor of sticking with a good thing, because the strategy is very important. I show you how to apply it in later chapters.

Golden Rule 3: Practise good money management with your share portfolio

Good money management means limiting your possible loss on any one share to a low proportion of your investment capital. Doing so means if the share price falls and you need to sell, your loss will be only a relatively small amount. Sounds pretty good, doesn't it? Indeed, it is very good and not a difficult strategy to apply.

> **Tip**
>
> In chapter 12, I provide a strategy that enables you to lose no more than 2% and preferably no more than 1% of your investing capital on any one share.

Golden Rule 4: Diversify your share investing capital

This rule to diversify your share investing capital among various different types of shares follows naturally from rule 3. If you want to limit your losses, you need to spread your capital about. You can't afford to risk investing all your capital on only one or two shares. If you do this and those shares turn out to be winners, great—you'll end up with a big profit. On the other hand, if only one turns out to be a loser, you could lose a large proportion of your investing capital. So the safest option is to spread your capital about.

Tip

Even if you have only as little as $2000 to invest, you can still buy four different shares in parcels of $500 each.

Golden Rule 5: Invest in good-quality shares

Invest most of your capital in 'good-quality' Australian-listed shares that pay a reasonable dividend—preferably fully franked.

The principle of investing in 'good-quality' shares is fairly self-explanatory. These types of shares are also known as *blue chip* shares and are shares in large, well-established businesses that have been around for a long time and have well-known and accepted products. They make good profits and distribute some of the profit back to shareholders in the form of dividends. Many of them are so-called household names, meaning most Australians recognise the name of the company or the product. These companies have very little chance of 'going under' and can be expected to continue profitable operations into the foreseeable future.

Tip

In the next chapter, I give you some examples of what I consider 'quality' Australian shares.

Golden Rule 6: Look towards the future with shares

I realise you have had a lot of rules to think about so I won't burden you with any more other than this final one: Look towards the future with shares.

The sharemarket is forward looking and share prices depend far more on future prospects than past performance. No matter how good profits were in the past, these profits can't flow into your investment account in the future. Thinking that past performance will always continue into the future is a mistake. Performance may well continue but it may well not. Certainly, you can use the past as a guide to the future, but remember that it's only a guide.

You can picture this approach very much like driving a car, where your main focus is on what's going on ahead but every now and then you look in the rear-view mirror to see what's going on behind.

Tip

Beware of basing your share decisions solely on future or 'blue sky' potential. Share prices driven up by blue sky potential usually involve lots of 'hype'. They're also known as 'bubbles' because they can rise up quickly but might be pricked at any time when commonsense kicks in.

Key takeaways

- Shares are a very convenient form of investment that you can easily get in to or out of, and at low cost.

- You can reduce the risk associated with shares by taking a longer term view and by diversifying and practising good money management.

- Lots of benefits are associated with share investing. These include flexibility, low trading cost, high rate of return, diversity, no holding cost or hassles and taxation benefits.

- Try to base your share decisions on rational considerations rather than emotions.

- Try to avoid panic buying or selling, and beware of psychological traps such as FOMO, FOL and confirmation bias.

- If you're on to a winner, stick to it. However, if your investment turns sour, it's usually best to get out and limit your losses.

- The sharemarket is driven primarily by what the future may hold rather than what's occurred in the past. The past can be a good guide to the future but you can't make profits retrospectively.

Chapter 6

Sectors and shares for your portfolio

I start this chapter by explaining two key terms used with shares — namely, market capitalisation (market cap) and liquidity. I then describe market and industry sectors and their importance to you as a share investor. Finally, I suggest some Australian listed shares you may want to consider for your core portfolio.

Because around 2000 shares are listed with the ASX, obviously I can consider only a handful of them in this chapter.

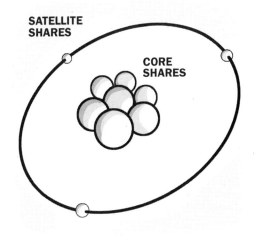

The shares I suggest here are in stable Australian companies, so they're suitable for the core of a longer term, lower risk share portfolio. They have a history of good dividends and capital gains, and there's every likelihood that these should continue into the future. I won't discuss speculative shares, which could be more suitable as satellites for a small proportion of your investing capital.

This approach to a share portfolio is known as a core and satellite approach.

Tip

Because changes occur continually with shares, you need to assess each of my suggestions in this chapter for suitability at the time you're setting up your portfolio. Please regard my suggestions as general advice and not recommendations. Certainly don't invest in any company before you've done your own research and come to your own conclusions.

Understanding two key terms

Two key terms become important as we start to get into the nitty-gritty of investing in shares. These are market capitalisation and liquidity.

Market capitalisation

As you'd expect, shares vary in popularity. One way of measuring their 'popularity' is by looking at the number of shareholders. However, this isn't a very good way because shares vary greatly in price. A better guide to the popularity of a share is the amount of money invested in it. This is known as *market capitalisation*, often shortened to *market cap*. Market cap is calculated using the following formula:

$$\text{Market cap} = \text{number of shares} \times \text{share price}$$

Shares with a high market cap are usually those that have a high price. For example, some shares trade for around $100 or more and they'll have a high market cap—sometimes in the billions of dollars. Other shares may trade for only a few cents and will have a low market cap, measured in millions of dollars. The shares I consider 'good quality' ones usually have a high market cap.

Because market cap depends on the share price as well as the number of issued shares, it changes as share prices change. If a share price rises, market cap increases; if the price falls, market cap decreases. This is because the number of issued shares changes only if new shares are issued or existing shares are bought back by the company and withdrawn from the market. Neither of these events occurs very often, although the number of shares

HIGH MARKET CAP   LOW MARKET CAP

can increase somewhat every six months if the company has a dividend reinvestment plan (DRP) in place.

Liquidity

Liquidity is a term used to describe the ease at which shares can be traded. Liquid shares are easy to trade because heaps of trades in these shares occur each day, so you won't have any problems if you want to trade them. Usually liquid shares have a small *spread*—that is, the price difference between buyers and sellers. (I expand on this concept in chapter 10).

Illiquid shares don't trade often, meaning they can be more difficult to trade when you want to and the spread can be large. Sometimes the delay between placing an order and the order transacting (if it does) can be several days.

High market cap shares are usually very liquid, but some of the not-so-well-known shares can be illiquid.

Tip

Another good reason for sticking to quality shares for your core portfolio is because they're liquid and easy to trade.

Considering sectors

The Australian sharemarket (or indeed any sharemarket), can be divided into sectors. The two main types of sectors, and so ways of dividing the market, are:

- industry sectors
- market sectors.

Industry sectors

Industry sectors divide the Australian sharemarket according to the type of business a company is in. In this way, the sharemarket is similar to a cake divided into slices, where each slice is a sector consisting of shares in the same type of business. As you'd expect, the slices will be of different sizes because each sector has a different market cap. For example, in Australia, the financial sector is a big slice of the market because the major banks and financial institutions are popular with investors and their shares usually trade at a relatively high price.

The main industry sectors are shown in figure 6.1.

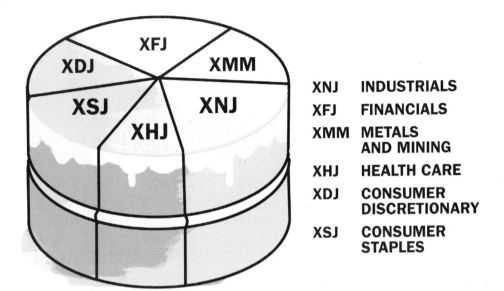

XNJ	**INDUSTRIALS**
XFJ	**FINANCIALS**
XMM	**METALS AND MINING**
XHJ	**HEALTH CARE**
XDJ	**CONSUMER DISCRETIONARY**
XSJ	**CONSUMER STAPLES**

Figure 6.1: Industry sectors divide the market according to business type

Tip

Figure 6.1 simply provides an idea of Australian sectors so don't interpret it too literally. Not all Australian industry sectors are shown, and the sectors aren't drawn to scale according to market cap.

Market sectors

A market sector is obtained by ranking shares according to their market cap and grouping them accordingly. Each differently sized group is known as an *index* and given a three-letter code that starts with an 'X'. Because a market index is based on market cap and market cap in turn depends on the share price, shares can move in to or out of an index as their price changes. For example, a recent addition to the top 20 index was Afterpay, which wasn't in the index until December 2020 when the share price skyrocketed.

Some of the main Australian market indices are shown in table 6.1 (overleaf).

Table 6.1: The main Australian market indices

Code	Size (Market Cap)
XAO	500 largest
XKO	300 largest
XJO	200 largest
XTO	100 largest
XFL	50 largest
XTL	20 largest

Tip

If you want to know how the sharemarket is performing, following the largest market index—the All Ordinaries Index (known as XAO All Ords)—is best because it represents most investor dollars (usually 95% or more). However, even some of the smaller ones such as the XTO give a good indication of overall performance.

Share selection using a market index

The shares included in an index give you a good starting point for selecting shares for your portfolio. Obviously, a large index such as the XAO isn't very helpful because you'd need to troll through 500 different shares. However, a smaller one, such as the XTL with only 20 shares, is practical.

The makeup of the XTL at the time of writing is shown in table 6.2.

Table 6.2: Makeup of the XTL, July 2021

Code	Name	Sector
ALL	Aristocrat Leisure	Consumer Discretionary
ANZ	ANZ Bank	Financials
APT	Afterpay Ltd	Information Technology
BHP	BHP Group	Materials
CBA	Commonwealth Bank of Australia	Financials
CSL	CSL Ltd	Health Care
FMG	Fortescue Metals	Materials
GMG	Goodman Group	Real Estate
MQG	Macquarie Group	Financials
NAB	National Australia Bank	Financials
NCM	Newcrest Mining	Materials
REA	REA Group	Communication Services
RIO	Rio Tinto	Materials
TCL	Transurban Group	Industrials
TLS	Telstra	Communication Services
WBC	Westpac Banking	Financials
WES	Wesfarmers	Consumer Discretionary
WOW	Woolworths	Consumer Staples
WPL	Woodside Petroleum	Energy
XRO	Xero	Technology

Note: In table 6.2, the shares are listed alphabetically and not in market cap order.

Tip

Your broker (either offline or online) should be able to provide you with a table of all shares included in an index.

Diversification

As shown in table 6.2, some of the shares in the top 20 index are in the same industry sector. If you want a diversified cross-section of shares, selecting shares from different industry sectors is a good idea. This rule has one exception—because in some cases you can get good diversification even with shares in the same industry sector. For example, in the materials sector, BHP, Fortescue, Newcrest and Rio Tinto are all included, yet the nature of their operations is very different. Newcrest is primarily concerned with gold whereas Fortescue is primarily in the iron ore business, and BHP and Rio Tinto have a more diversified range of products. So you may be able to get good diversification with companies in the same sector provided each company has different products.

Tip

Using a market index to select quality shares for your portfolio is a good approach and one I suggest you consider.

Sectors and shares you may want to consider

In this section, I outline my suggestions for sectors and shares in them that you can consider for your core portfolio. The shares I suggest are in what I consider to be quality, well-established Australian companies in each sector. Some of them are included in my own core share portfolio and some are included in the XTL (top 20) index.

Tip

I have faith in you and I'm sure you'll make good a good selection of shares for your portfolio using your own nous.

I have grouped my suggested core shares according to the sector the company is in, as follows:

- listed investment companies and exchange-traded funds

- banks and financial institutions

- mineral and oil companies

- retailers

- real estate

- health care

- other well-established and profitable businesses.

Note: When I list a share in the following sections, I also include its ASX code in brackets.

Listed investment companies and exchange-traded funds

These companies don't have a product of their own but invest in other businesses. The difference between a listed investment company (LIC) and an exchange-traded fund (ETF) is basically in the structure of the business. As an investor, however, this will make no significant difference to you. Both types are listed on the ASX, which means you can trade them in the same way as you would trade ordinary shares. You can choose between heaps of LICs and ETFs with differing investment styles. Some are general in nature and invest in a wide range of businesses, while others are more specialised—for example, they may concentrate on ethical investing or emerging companies, or on large (or small) companies operating in Australia or overseas. Some Australian LICs such as WHSP (SOL), Australian Foundation Investment Company (AFI), Argo (ARG) and Platinum Capital (PMC)—just to name a few—have been around for a long time and are well established.

The beauty of investing in LICs and ETFs is that you get a great deal of diversification with just one share. A single LIC or managed fund can give you exposure to a mixture of 20 or more Australian companies. Some LICs or ETFs also invest in international securities, so by purchasing their shares you can gain exposure to international markets without the hassle of trying to do so yourself.

> **Tip**
>
> I suggest you don't have just one LIC in your core portfolio but several of them with differing investing styles.

Banks and financial institutions

Over the years, Australian banks have received a great deal of media publicity—and most of this has been adverse. The threat of competition from other types of financial enterprise has also been raised. But despite it all, the banks have kept on keeping on and still generate good profits and pay worthwhile, fully franked dividends.

The Banking Royal Commission, conducted mainly during 2018, revealed a surprising number of shonky practices in the Australian financial sector the public previously hadn't known about. Consequently, most of the banks and some financial institutions received a sharp rap on the knuckles as well as large fines. This caused bank shares to dive. They were just recovering from this assault when the worldwide COVID-19 pandemic caused all sharemarkets to drop like lead balloons, and bank shares were dragged down in the backwash.

The COVID-19 threat hasn't adversely affected the economy to the extent it was first feared, so the future of banks and financial institutions is looking rosier again. They have cleaned up their act by tightening loan requirements and ensuring customers are given advice that's best for them, rather than what's best for the advisor or the bank. The large banks include the 'big four'—ANZ, CBA, NAB and Westpac (WBC)—as well as the major commercial bank Macquarie (MOQ), which continues to be a great performer. Some smaller banks also merit consideration, including Bank of Queensland (BOQ), Bendigo and Adelaide bank (BEN) and Suncorp (SUN), which is also a large insurance company. There has been talk of Suncorp divesting itself of banking operations and focusing wholly on insurance but so far this hasn't happened.

As well as the banks, some financial institutions are also worth considering. They're smaller than the major banks and somewhat more risky, but options include Mortgage Choice (MOC), Australian Financial Group (AFG) and Money Corporation (MNY), along with many others.

Tip

In my experience, banks and major financial institutions have generally been profitable longer term investments, so I suggest you include at least one in your core share portfolio. Apart from any other considerations, these shares usually pay a substantial dividend that has the added bonus of being fully franked.

Mineral and oil companies

A huge number of mineral and oil companies are listed on the Australian sharemarket. Most of the smaller ones are simply explorers, but the larger ones are often producers as well. In my list of profitable ones, I consider only those that produce a commercially saleable product and have been in operation for many years. This includes BHP, Rio Tinto (RIO), Woodside (WPL), Santos (STO), Beach Petroleum (BPT), Newcrest (NCM), Fortescue Metals (FMG) and Iluka (ILU).

Many of the smaller and less well-established companies in this sector operate in rather unstable overseas countries and are yet to produce a saleable product or return a profit. That's to say, they operate at a loss. For these companies, you might wonder how long they can continue operating as they are chewing up funds every day. Nevertheless, some have been around for a considerable time. The upside to investing in an explorer is that if it does 'strike gold' (sometimes literally) and make a worthwhile discovery, the shares could skyrocket and you could make a large capital gain.

If you're considering investing in mineral and oil companies in the energy business, you need to factor in the ongoing trend in world energy demand. Coal and oil have been Australian stalwarts for many years, but the shift away from them is growing as world economies strive to reduce emissions that cause global warming. Gas is the cleanest of the fossil fuels but gas burning still produces greenhouse gas emissions—mainly carbon dioxide. Nuclear fission is a viable alternative for zero emission power production in large amounts but nuclear waste disposal is a problem. Also there is the danger of a power plant mishap with catastrophic results, as occurred in Chernobyl and Fukushima. These problems have deterred many countries from going nuclear. In Australia, some have suggested we should replace our coal-burning power stations with nuclear ones, but traditionally Australians have been very anti-nuclear.

The switch to renewable energy sources is undoubtedly increasing. Electricity is already being produced in large amounts from sunlight and wind in many countries, including Australia. The uptake of electric vehicles has been rapid, and this is driving global demand for rechargeable batteries (although Australia is somewhat of a laggard here). This, in turn, drives demand for minerals used in wind turbines, batteries and solar cells—including lithium, cobalt, nickel, manganese, graphite, alumina and tin—as well as rare-earth elements such as cerium, samarium, lanthanum and neodymium. Many small mining companies specialise in one or more of these metals, as well as an established Australian one—Iluka (ILU)—which is a major global supplier of zircon and titanium minerals and also has operations in Sierra Leone and Sir Lanka.

Tip

Some Australian listed mineral and oil companies have overseas operations and may not pay full Australian tax on their profits. This means any dividends paid may be unfranked or not fully franked. So it's a good idea to first check the franking on the dividend (if there is one) before investing.

Retailers

Retailers provide products and advice to consumers. In most cases, they don't produce the products they sell, although in some cases they do value-add. For example, some supermarkets have bakeries and also make products such as specialist salads. Also, the trend toward generic supermarket products has been increasing. These products carry the supermarket brand but aren't actually made by them—they're products made by others that have simply been repackaged and rebranded.

You're no doubt familiar with most of the well-established retailers—including Woolworths (WOW), Coles (COL), Harvey Norman (HVN), JB Hi-Fi (JBH), Nick Scali (NCK) and others. The other Australian company behind many well-known retail operations is Metcash (MTS). However, Metcash is a more diversified business and as well as owning IGA supermarkets it also owns Mitre 10 and Home and Timber Hardware. I regard them as a more risky proposition because they're operating in a very competitive environment and haven't yet been able to capture a significant market share.

Of the retailers listed, I consider Woolworths to be the most reliable. Over many years, Woolworths has been at the forefront of the supermarket business and has rewarded shareholders with appreciable fully franked dividends and a generally increasing share price driven by steady profits. Woolworths previously owned a large number of poker machines and were also into liquor retailing (through the BWS chain), but these parts of the business were shed off in 2021 and are now an independent listed company, Endeavour (EDV).

Coles has been a steady competitor to Woolworths. Previously owned by Wesfarmers, it was spun off in 2018 and is now an independent listed company (COL). Coles is still involved with liquor retailing as it owns Liquorland and Vintage Cellars.

Tip

Unfortunately, as mentioned in chapter 2, some profitable retailers such as Aldi and Bunnings aren't public or separately listed companies so you can't buy shares directly in them. However, you can get a slice of the action at Bunnings by investing in Wesfarmers (WES), because Bunnings is fully owned by them.

Real estate investment companies

Real estate has generally been a very good investment in Australia but, as I note in chapter 5, investing directly in property has some formidable problems for an investor. A viable alternative is buying shares in a real estate investment company, because this allows you to get a slice of the action with a small amount of capital. You have heaps of listed real estate investment companies to choose from (85 at the time of writing). They're also known as *real estate investment trusts*, or REITs.

The larger well-established listed REITs include Goodman Group (GMG— included in the XTL index), Scentre (SCG), Stockland (SGP), Dexus (DXS), Mirvac (MGR), Lendlease (LLC), GPT Group (GPT), Vicinity Centres (VCX) and Carter Hall Group (CHC).

Tip

While Australian property has generally been a good long-term investment, share REITs haven't always proved to be a good investment. The best property investment in Australia has been in land, homes and home units, whereas many REITs are more into commercial property. The dividend is often unfranked or partly franked so you need to check this and the investment profile before investing.

Health care

Health care companies supply or produce pharmaceuticals and health care equipment and services. Some quality health care companies have been operating in Australia for a long time, and shares in these companies have proved to be good investments. The standouts are Commonwealth Serum Laboratories (CSL), Blackmores (BKL), Cochlear (COH) and Resmed (RMD).

You might also want to consider others (some with a somewhat more chequered history) such as Mayne Pharma (MYX), Ramsay Health Care (RHC) and Sonic Health Care (SHL), along with smaller players such as Ansell (ANN) and Sigma (SIG).

Other quality businesses

The companies I have mentioned so far are by no means a complete list of suitable companies you can consider for inclusion in your core portfolio. Many other well-established and profitable companies listed on the Australian sharemarket are well worth consideration.

These include Telstra (TLS), Australian Securities Exchange (ASX) and Tabcorp (TAH), as well as many others. Some of the smaller and more speculative companies offer the promise of good future profits if their product can be successfully brought to market, Again, just keep in mind they're a more risky proposition and more suitable as satellites rather than core shares.

Key takeaways

- The best measure of the popularity of a share with investors is its *market cap*, which is the share price multiplied by the number of issued shares.

- Quality shares usually have a high market cap and speculative shares usually have a low market cap.

- *Liquidity* is the term used to describe how often a share is traded and, therefore, how easy it is to buy or sell when you want to. With liquid shares the spread is usually small.

- Liquid shares should have little time delay between placing an order and the order transacting, whereas illiquid shares could have a considerable time delay.

- Quality shares are usually very liquid.

- The Australian sharemarket can be divided into groups according to industry sectors or market sectors.

- An industry sector consists of shares grouped according to the type of business they're in, whereas a market sector (or market index) groups shares according to their popularity (as measured by market cap).

- By choosing shares included in a market index, you have a good starting point for a core portfolio. To be practical, you need to use an index with a relatively small number of shares, such as the XTL (20 shares), XFL (50 shares) or XTO (100 shares).

- I've included some suggestions for sectors and shares in them that you might like to consider for your core portfolio, but remember—they're just my suggestions. Use your own discretion and judgement before making any decisions about shares to include in your portfolio.

Chapter 7

Setting up to trade

Even if you're going to be a long-term investor, you need to be able to *trade* shares — that is, buy or sell them when you want. You need to purchase shares to set up your portfolio in the first place and, after that, you may need to re-jig your portfolio by trading shares as time goes on. Even if you're a long-term investor, you may also like to have a sporting flutter on a few speckies, and that will involve trading them more frequently.

In this chapter, I first run through some common reasons for wanting (or needing) to buy or sell shares, and then show you how you can set up to trade, using either an offline or online broker, so that when the time comes you'll be able to take action. I also describe the CHESS system and why you should join it.

Note: I discuss the 'nuts and bolts' of trading shares and the types of orders you can place in chapter 10.

Tip

Blindly following the advice of others to trade shares isn't usually a good move.

'Buy some now! I reckon these shares will do well.'

Reasons for wanting to trade shares

Some of the main reasons you might want to buy shares are:

- You have some savings that aren't earning much in interest and you want to put your spare cash to work.

- You receive a windfall from a tax refund, inheritance, lottery win or other source and you'd like to invest the funds in shares.

- You get a tip about shares from a friend, relative, hairdresser, media article or some other source and you feel it's a good tip you'd like to act on.

The main reasons you might want to sell shares are:

- You want to convert some of your shares into cash because you need the money.

- You own some shares that are underperforming and you want to sell them and re-invest the funds in other shares you think could be better performers. (That is, you want to re-jig your portfolio.)

- You own some shares where the price is falling and you want to sell them should the price fall to your stop limit.

Tip

As already mentioned, selling underperforming shares is usually a difficult psychological hurdle. However, the sooner you get over it, the better. Try to take the emotion out of the decision and treat a sale as just another trade.

Deciding between offline and online trading

Before you start looking for a broker, you need to make a major decision—are you going to trade offline or online?

Offline trading

You trade offline by becoming a client of an offline broker you can communicate with and who'll trade on your behalf. Your communication may be by phone or text message, or any other mutually agreed on way. If the broker has an office conveniently located, you might want to go there and make personal contact—particularly during the initial stage of setting up. At the same time, you could complete the necessary paperwork during this visit. Otherwise, you can have the paperwork mailed or emailed to

'Which path should I take?'

you. To complete the process, you'll need to provide identification, bank details and tax file number.

If you decide to trade offline, you'll need to make another major decision — are you going to use a broker who gives advice or one who gives no advice and simply follows your instructions? Naturally, a broker who gives no advice will be cheaper than a broker who gives advice. The downside of using the 'no advice' option is you won't be able to discuss any ideas you have with the broker. So if you want your broker to be a knowledgeable person you can talk to about your planned trades and will then provide their advice, you need to use a broker who gives advice. You can also consider using the services of a financial advisor who's knowledgeable about shares.

Certainly, wanting to talk to a knowledgeable person before you trade is understandable, especially if you're a novice to the sharemarket. But before you start paying for advice, I caution you to consider that the advice you receive from a broker or financial advisor isn't necessarily going to lead to any better decisions than the ones you make using your own nous. The recent Banking Royal Commission uncovered evidence that, in many cases, the advice given by brokers and financial advisors was based more on their own self-interest than that of their clients.

You can also take your share trading decisions a degree further by using the services of a broker or financial advisor who offers a *full service*. In this case, virtually everything is done for you — including selecting the shares in your portfolio, trading on your behalf, setting up the account, making the financial transactions, keeping track of your portfolio and reporting back to you. If you decide to go this route, you basically don't have to do anything other than read the reports that will periodically be provided for you. Naturally, this is the most costly option and I don't recommend it.

Wanting to talk to someone about the market and shares you own or those you're considering purchasing is just human nature. Rather than paying a broker or financial advisor, however, you may be able to find an interested friend or relative you can chat with about shares. Another option is to join an online shares forum (also known as a *chat room*). This doesn't cost anything and allows you to post and receive messages about shares from others interested in them. Quite a few different Australian-based options are available, including Hotcopper (hotcopper.com.au), which has been around for a long time.

> ## Tip
>
> I've written this book to give you the knowledge and confidence you need to make your own decisions about shares and be able to manage your portfolio. I presume you're reading it to acquire the knowledge and confidence you need to be self-sufficient.

Offline orders

If you decide to trade offline, you'll need to contact your broker whenever you're considering a trade. This contact is usually by phone but sometimes you can use a text message or email. You'll then advise the broker of the details of your proposed trade. If you're using a broker who gives advice, you'll no doubt ask your broker for suggestions before the proposed trade is finalised.

A dialogue with an offline broker who provides advice might go something like this:

YOU: I've just received a tax refund of $4000 that I'd like to invest in shares. What do you suggest?

BROKER: I'm currently recommending ACME shares because I think they're a good buy at the moment.

YOU: What are they trading for?

BROKER: Let me check. *[Pause.]* Last trade was $1.54.

YOU: So how many could I buy?

BROKER: With $4000 you could buy … 2560 shares, taking into account brokerage.

YOU: Okay. Please go ahead and buy them at the best price.

BROKER: Okay, will do and I'll let you know after the trade goes ahead.

Online trading

You trade online by becoming a customer with an online broker. To do this, you first need to comply with the broker's requirements for new customers, including providing 100 points of identification, your tax file number

(TFN) and details of a cash account where the broker can withdraw funds for a purchase trade or deposit them for a sell trade. You'll also need to nominate your preferred password for approval. In some cases, online brokers have a dedicated cash account linked to their trading platform, and they'll then usually provide financial incentives for you to use this account rather than one of your own.

'Wow! Now I'm a customer and I can trade!'

Once you've jumped through these hoops and are accepted as a customer, you're ready to start trading.

Once your account is finalised, your broker will allocate several numbers to you, including:

- account number and/or log-in code

- CHESS number (see later in this chapter for more on CHESS)

- trading account number if you're using the broker's account for cash transfers

- trading pin—allocated in some cases for added security; you'll need to quote this pin for each order before the broker will execute the trade.

Tip

You can see that online trading creates quite a few numbers as well as a password to keep track of. I suggest you don't trust your memory! Instead, write down the numbers and codes and keep them in a secure place—not a computer or smart phone that possibly could be hacked.

Online orders

Once you're accepted as a customer, you can trade online using the broker's trading platform. To do this, you log in to the site using your user details and follow the prompts. When all details of your planned order are completed, the broker will most likely summarise the proposed trade and the net cost or revenue involved. You'll then need to confirm that all details are correct and, if you do so, the broker will send your order to market.

Pros and cons of investing online

Online investing has some advantages and disadvantages. The advantages include:

- You're in complete control.

- You'll develop your expertise as you get more familiar with the procedures.

- Online trading is cheaper than offline trading.

- The cheaper brokerage makes trading small-value parcels a feasible proposition.

- Heaps of free info is available.

- You can access charts and tables—usually much easier to digest than spoken info.

- You can research on your broker's website at any time of the day or night.

- You can experiment and test ideas or systems online without cost—provided you don't confirm a trade.

- You can place orders using any convenient device that allows you to connect to the web, including your computer, mobile phone or even smart watch.

- The time delay between placing and completing the order in the market is very small because devices that connect to the internet do so very quickly.

- Many online trading sites provide recommendations and also may have a chat room included in their site.

The disadvantages of online investing include:

- You can't discuss your investing ideas with a knowledgeable broker.

- You need a degree of computer and internet literacy—but this shouldn't really be much of a problem (especially after you've finished reading this book).

- Hacking is a small but possible risk.

Tip

If you're not confident about investing online straightaway, you could start by using an offline broker and then gradually convert to the online method later on.

Finding a broker

If you decide on the offline broker route, you might want to find a broker or financial advisor conveniently located. However, communication nowadays by mobile phone or email is so fast and inexpensive that location isn't usually an important consideration. A good starting point for finding a broker or financial advisor is the bank you use for your financial transactions. The bank will almost certainly have a financial advisor or be able to suggest one who'll be able to offer various levels of service with regard to shares.

If you decide to take the online route, you could also start off with the bank you're a customer with. All major Australian banks have online trading platforms (or are linked to one), and they'll be able to advise you of the procedure to follow to become a customer. This is especially valuable because you may be able to link your share trading account to your existing accounts with the bank. Also, by logging in to their internet trading site, you should be able to access all your accounts (including your share trading account) with one click of the button.

The most popular trading site in Australia is CommSec (commsec.com.au), which is a subsidiary of the Commonwealth Bank. Because of this, I've used this site in all my examples in this book. In my opinion, it's a good all-round site that's relatively user-friendly. If you're interested in this site, you need to access it directly because it's an independent company. This means you can get only limited advice about the site from a Commonwealth Bank branch. Most likely, the bank staff will just give you a phone number to call.

Tip

If you want to delve deeper into the various online trading sites, please refer to my book *Online Investing on the Australian Sharemarket*, now in its fifth edition. Another good way of finding a broker is from a web search. The Finder site (www.finder.com.au) is a very good one that you can use to research both online and offline brokers.

Online facilities

If you decide to use an online trading platform, it can be difficult to decide on which one without actually using the site. You can easily get bogged down if you try to troll through all the sites trying to find the cheapest or 'best' one. I deliberately put the word 'best' in inverted commas here, because it's very difficult for you to specify what you want from an online site until you get more experienced, and so have a better idea of what you really want—or don't want.

Some of the differences between the various online sites are of value only for experienced traders who may seek more sophisticated trading platforms or more detailed information than what you'll want (at least initially). I've found the various online sites don't really offer much difference that will be of importance to you. The competition

'How can I choose which one is best for me when I don't really know what I want?'

is quite intense, so the sites have to offer similar rates and options if they want to maintain market share. Trading fees may be different between the various online sites but because brokerage is so low, this shouldn't be an important consideration unless you plan to make heaps of trades — and as an investor you shouldn't want to do that.

So you really don't need to agonise too much about your selection and, instead, just get started. Remember that you don't need to have only one online broker — you can become a customer with several and chop and choose as you please and compare features as you get more experienced. The only proviso is that you must keep track of the trades you make with each broker. That's to say, you can't buy shares using broker A and sell the same shares later on using broker B.

Can you see why?

The answer is that each broker gives you a different Holder Identification Number (covered in the next section). This means you can't sell using a different broker from the one you bought the shares through, unless you've previously arranged to have the shares transferred using a broker to broker transfer form.

Tip

Setting up an account with a broker may take some time and perhaps a few phone calls to overcome any problems that may arise. So it's good to get your broker sorted fairly early in the piece.

Understanding CHESS

Here's something important I need to explain and it's not about the age-old board game. CHESS is an acronym that stands for Clearing House Electronic Sub-register System. Wow! That's a mouthful, but now I've told you what it means you can forget it. All you need to know is that CHESS was set up to make life easier for everyone in the share trading game — including you.

When you set up to trade with a broker, either offline or online, you're given the option of joining CHESS with that broker. If you do so, your broker will sponsor you into the system. (Naturally enough, this is known as broker sponsorship.) You're then given a unique CHESS number that remains the same for all your trades with that broker. This number is known as a Holder Identification Number (HIN). If you decide you'd like to trade with another broker, you'll need to get another HIN for all your trades with that broker. Therefore, if you trade with more than one broker, you need to keep track of which shares were traded with each one.

When you buy shares, you're issued with a CHESS holding statement for those shares using your HIN with that broker. If you sell any shares or add to your holding at any time, you'll receive a new CHESS statement. All this and it won't cost you a cent. So you don't need to mull over the decision—just do it!

Before CHESS came along, another system (which is still available) was used. This was called *issuer sponsorship* because the share issuer allocated a number to you that applied to those shares only. This number was called the Shareholder Reference Number (SRN). If you bought some different shares, they carried another SRN—even if you used the same broker for the trade. This meant that if you held a number of different shares, you had a different SRN for each one. What a hassle, all those numbers to keep track of! So forget this method and just go with CHESS!

Tip

If by some means or other you own some shares that still carry the issuer sponsorship number, you can convert them to CHESS. Simply contact your broker (online or offline), who'll do it free of charge.

Key takeaways

- You might want to buy shares for several reasons. Underlying all of them, the main reason is because you want to put your money to work and earn more than you can get from depositing it in a low interest account.

- You might also want to sell shares for several reasons, but the main reason underlying them should be that the shares are underperforming or are in a downtrend price mode. You shouldn't sell shares when the price is rising unless you desperately need the money.

- You can trade offline or online depending on your personal preference. I urge you to seriously consider the online option because it has heaps of advantages.

- If you trade offline, three levels of service should be available—namely, no advice, advice or full service. Naturally, as you move up the scale, the charges increase.

- Australian banks have online trading platforms or are linked to one. Using the trading platform offered by the bank you use for your finances is a good starting point.

- The Finder site is a very good one that lists many online and offline Australian brokers and provides some comparison information.

- The various online broking sites do have some differences, including in the information available and in their fee structures. These differences are really not significant for any but very experienced traders. For you, the similarities are more important than the differences so spending too much time trying to find the 'best' broker isn't worthwhile.

- CHESS is a wonderful system that gives you just one number to keep track of for all your trades with a broker. And it doesn't cost a cent!

Chapter 8

Getting to know your shares

As I've already stated several times, if you're going to invest in shares you need to know them. Buying shares on an emotional whim such as FOMO isn't a good idea, and you also shouldn't blindly follow the advice of others—no matter how qualified they may be or how much experience they've had.

You can easily access heaps of info about shares, so you can get all the info you need to make informed decisions. The trick is not to get bogged down with a lot of info you don't really need. In this chapter, I guide you through gathering the important info you need about shares—known as *fundamental analysis*—and how you can get it and make sense of it.

Using fundamental analysis

Getting the basic info about shares is known as completing *fundamental analysis*. The info you need is:

- general info
- financial info.

General info

General info is the basic data about the company you're interested in. When you have checked this out, you should know the answer to each of the following six questions:

- What does the company do—what are its saleable products?

- How well known is the company or its products?

- How long has the company been operating?

- How large is the company?

- How much competition does the company have?

- How long is the company likely to continue operating?

Tip

Answering these six questions does not provide a complete list of fundamentals applying to a business, but will give you a pretty good idea. When considering these questions, you don't need to be precise but you do need to have some idea.

What does the company do—what are its saleable products?

In chapter 5, I provide the example of the faithful followers of Elon Musk losing lots of money because they bought shares in a company simply because they thought he had recommended it. To avoid this type of mistake, you need to make sure you understand the company and its products before you press the 'buy' button on its shares. I suggest you follow the advice of Warren Buffett—who's generally acknowledged as the world's most successful company director and share investor—when he said that he never invests in a business if he doesn't really understand what it does or how it makes a profit.

The products of a company can be of two basic types:

- *Goods or materials you can get your hands on.* For example, products such as cars or whitegoods (including refrigerators and washing machines), or mined products such as iron ore or crude oil.

- *Services that you can't actually get your hands on.* A service is something a company does for a customer that they need but can't do (or don't want to do) for themselves. For example, Qantas provides aerial transportation for customers but Qantas doesn't make planes or any other hardware connected with aviation. Similarly, retailers don't usually make the products they sell but provide a service by offering goods for sale as well as giving advice and possible credit to customers if needed.

Tip

If you still don't really understand the company or its products after doing your research—stay away. I suggest you apply this well-known saying: If in doubt, stay out!

How well known is the company or its products?

Does the business or its products have some well-known brand identification? In Australia, many well-known companies or products are 'household names'. This includes most of the banks, large retailers and other businesses such as Arnott's and Akubra, or products such as Vegemite and Tim Tams.

Tip

Investing in companies that are well known and established is generally safer. However, just because a business or its products aren't well known doesn't necessarily mean you should stay away. The company could be exploiting a profitable niche in the market (and so be very well known to certain customers) and the shares could be a good investment.

How long has the company been operating?

The company might just be floating and their shares on offer in the form of an IPO. In this situation, no operating history as a public company is available or track record for the shares. At the other the extreme, the company could have been operating in Australia for decades with a long shares history.

Clearly the longer the company has been operating profitably, the lower the risk of unexpected earnings blips.

Tip

I suggest you avoid the temptation of subscribing to an IPO and wait until the shares have been on the market for some time. This enables you to get an idea of the share price action. If the share price rises on listing, you'll miss some of the initial profit but you'll also miss the loss should the share price dive.

How large is the company?

A large company is likely to have a number of branches or depots in Australia, employ a large number of personnel and have a large turnover (sales revenue). From a shareholder's point of view (and as discussed in chapter 6), the best measure of the size of a company is the *market cap*—that is, the total dollar value of its shares. In general, large market cap shares are the safest and best for your core portfolio.

Tip

Sometimes a small, profitable company can become a likely 'takeover target' and so a takeover bid is made for it. This is usually good news for shareholders because the share price in the smaller company usually rises.

How much competition does the company have?

In Australia, all businesses operate in competitive environments. Sometimes, however, a business may be relatively immune from competition—if, for example, it holds patents for its products or the company has established brand identification. You need to consider not only the company's current level of competition but also the possibility of increased competition in the future that could have an impact on profits.

> **Tip**
>
> Going with companies where there's little threat of increased competition affecting profitability is generally safer.

How long is the company likely to continue operating?

To answer this question, you need to do a bit of crystal-ball gazing—because you need to think about the likely future of the company and its products. What was successful in the past isn't necessarily going to be so in the future. You also need to consider any likely changes in legislation that could have an impact on the business.

For example, companies in the gaming or liquor business continually face the threat of increased government regulation. On the other hand, for some businesses a relaxation of government restrictions is possible, such as those in medicinal cannabis.

> **Tip**
>
> If you're setting up a longer term core portfolio, investing in companies with no major threats on the horizon is best. This means the company is likely to continue being profitable for the foreseeable future.

SWOT analysis

At this stage of your research, you might want to consider doing a SWOT analysis. SWOT stands for **s**trengths, **w**eaknesses, **o**pportunities and **t**hreats. The process is a well-known way of analysing the basics of a situation—in this case, a business—and getting some idea of how the future is likely to unfold.

> **Tip**
>
> A SWOT analysis may be worth considering at the early stages of your research into a business.

Financial info

You can access many financial statistics about shares, but here I simplify what's available for you by outlining only the really essential aspects.

Before I do so, however, a quick reminder. Naturally, you can access only the financial data that's made available but, unfortunately, this can't always be relied on. Companies have been known to sometimes use 'creative accounting'—where accountants 'massage the books' to disguise any bad news or pump up any good news. This practice has a long history, with author Mark Twain once proclaiming, 'There are three kinds of lies: lies, damned lies and statistics'.

Tip

You'll sometimes find an apparently profitable business with good-looking financial stats that the directors are talking up—but its share price is falling. This indicates some bad news is on the horizon that someone knows something about but which hasn't yet been revealed to the general public. So beware!

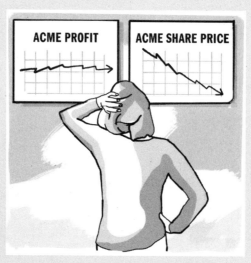

'There's something fishy going on!'

Profit (earnings)

The most important financial statistic of all is profit (or earnings). The main reason a business exists in an economy such as Australia's is to make a profit. The hard, cruel fact is that an unprofitable business can't survive indefinitely—unless the government or the shareholders are prepared to prop it up. Ask yourself, 'Why would anyone want to invest in a company that doesn't make a profit and is most likely never to do so?' Unprofitable companies that aren't government owned exist only because the shareholders think there's the prospect of future profitability (known as *blue sky* potential).

Let's look at the fundamental question of how a company makes a profit. The answer is that all companies have products—either goods or services—that are purchased by their customers. This provides dollar revenue. All businesses also have costs—also known as *expenses*—and these include payments for purchases, wages to staff and overhead costs such as government charges and depreciation. As shown in figure 8.1, the company makes a profit when the sales revenue is greater than the expenses; otherwise, it operates at a loss.

$$\text{Profit} = \text{total revenue} - \text{total expenses}$$

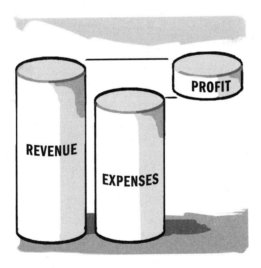

Figure 8.1: Total revenue minus expenses equals profit

Tip

A company that isn't making a profit is a more risky investment proposition.

Capital

All businesses require a money pool, known as *operating capital*. Initially, this capital comes from the shareholders but, as the business continues operating, the pool of capital changes (unless the revenue and expenses should exactly balance). If revenue is greater than expenses, capital increases. This is good news and means that the business has some excess capital it can use in many ways, including paying a dividend to shareholders. However, if there's no revenue, or the revenue is less than the expenses, capital diminishes. If this continues, the business will eventually run out of money and become bankrupt and the shares will become worthless.

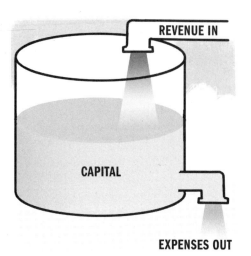

You can picture capital as water in a tank where water flows in and flows out. If the inflow matches the outflow, the level stays the same. If it's greater, the level rises, and if it's less or non-existent, the level falls until eventually the tank runs dry. This is equivalent to a business becoming bankrupt because it has run out of money.

Earnings per share

As a shareholder (or prospective shareholder), you can't really get a good picture of how profitable a company is simply from knowing it made *x* million or billion dollars profit. You need to measure the profit against a benchmark. For example, you'd expect a really big bank such as the Commonwealth Bank to make more profit than a smaller player such as the Bank of Queensland, simply because it's much larger.

A more meaningful statistic than dollar profit, therefore, is the *earnings per share*, or EPS. This is calculated by dividing the total earnings of the business by the total number of issued shares. This tells you how much profit is attributable to each share and so brings the profit figure more into perspective.

As a simple example, imagine a company makes a profit of $10 million and has 100 million issued shares. What is the EPS?

The EPS will be $10 000 000 ÷ 100 000 000 = $0.1 per share or 10¢.

Earnings trend

As well as looking at current and past earnings, considering the *trend* in earnings is also most important. Investors love to see that earnings have grown in the past and are projected to continue growing into the future. Investors hate earnings downgrades and if these are announced, the share price is usually punished — often more than the downgrade deserves.

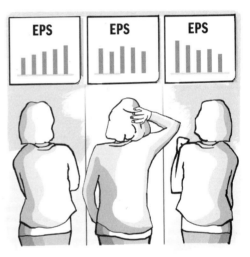

In your research, you need to check the trend in the EPS and whether any falls have occurred — and, if so, the reason for them. Also check to see if the company forecasts future earnings downgrades, or whether financial analysts are predicting they could be likely.

'There are great shares, okay shares and not okay shares.'

Return on capital

In chapter 1, I explain the importance of return on capital invested for your investments, and in chapter 3 I show you how to calculate it. The same concept applies to companies. If you wanted to go into business and were looking for a suitable one to purchase, you'd want to know how the profit shapes up in relation to the price of the business. Clearly, the more expensive the business, the more profit you'd expect. To get this into perspective when comparing share investment options, you can consider the return on capital (ROC).

The ROC is obtained by dividing the annual earnings by the capital invested, and then converting this to a percentage by multiplying by 100.

For example, say you're considering a business where the asking price is $100 000 and the annual earnings is $25 000. What do you think of this?

In this case, your capital invested would be $100 000 and the return on capital would be:

$$\$25\,000 \div \$100\,000 = 0.25$$

Now multiply 0.25 by 100 to get 25%.

That's a high return on capital invested, so you'd no doubt conclude this is a good investment option.

When considering ROC for your share investing, keep the following in mind:

- For a listed company, you don't need to calculate the ROC because it will be shown in the published key financial statistics.

- Capital invested isn't the same as market cap. Market cap depends on the share price but the capital invested in a company doesn't change even if the share price changes.

- The ROC is of little significance in the banking sector because most of the assets of a bank are in the form of loans to customers, so the ROC is historically low.

Tip

I consider 10% as a minimum acceptable ROC, but the higher the better. It's most desirable that the ROC should show a history of past growth with no appreciable downward blips (unless due to uncontrollable events such as COVID-19), and that the ROC is expected to rise in the future (or at least not fall).

Return on equity

Return on equity (ROE) is very similar to ROC, except that shareholder equity is used instead of capital invested. Shareholder equity is also known as *proprietorship* and it is the capital invested by the shareholders plus reserves. Reserves are the capital ploughed back into the business from accumulated past profits. You don't need to worry about the technical details of the calculation, because the ROE will also be shown in the published key financial statistics. The main reason I've mentioned ROE is because it's an often quoted statistic you'll probably come across.

> ## Tip
>
> Shareholder equity is less than capital invested, so ROE should be higher than ROC. If ROC should be at least 10%, you could expect ROE to be at least 12%.

Price to earnings ratio

The price to earnings ratio (PE or sometimes PER) is an important earnings statistic you need to get your head around. It's obtained by dividing the share price by the EPS, where both share price and EPS are in the same units—either dollars or cents.

For example, if a share price is $1.80 and the EPS is 10¢, what is the PE?

Using dollar units for both, the EPS is $0.10

So the PE is $1.80 ÷ $0.10 = 18

You can also calculate the PE by dividing the share price in cents by the EPS in cents. This calculation is 180 ÷ 10 = 18, which is of course the same answer.

> ## Tip
>
> You shouldn't need to calculate PE because it should be included in the available financial data.

INTERPRETING THE PE

The PE is a very useful earnings statistic because it relates earnings to share price. This gives you a way of comparing shares of different companies on an apples-to-apples basis, regardless of their size. For example, Commonwealth Bank (CBA) is a far larger player than Bendigo Bank (BEN). Yet when I check the PEs for each, I find that at the time of writing, the PE of CBA is 22.2 and that of BEN is 22.7. In other words, they're very similar statistics despite the size difference of the companies and the fact that the CBA share price is about 10 times the price of BEN!

The PE really tells you how long it takes to pay back a share from the earnings. A PE of 22 means that it would take 22 years to pay back the cost of this share from the earnings per share. You now have an idea of how 'cheap' or 'expensive' a share is—the higher the PE, the more 'expensive' the share because the longer it takes to pay for the share from the earnings. Because the PEs of CBA and BEN are almost the same, from a shareholder's point of view, the shares in both banks are fairly evenly valued by investors.

Tip

If no PE is shown in the financial data for a share, the company isn't making a profit—it's operating at a loss. Theoretically, the PE for a company making a loss would be negative, but negative values of the PE aren't usually shown. So if no PE value is given, you can assume the company is operating at a loss.

DECIDING ON A REASONABLE PE

When you're thinking about investing in shares, the real question relating to PE is, 'What's a reasonable PE?' In other words, should you look to buy a cheap share with a low PE, or an expensive one with a high PE?

At the time of writing, the average PE of ASX-listed shares is 22.7, so that gives you a benchmark value. The average market PE varies from time to time—in the past, for example, it has been as low as 10 or as high as 25. Everyone likes a bargain, so it's natural to think that low PE shares would be the best buy. Before you rush out and buy a heap of low PE shares, however, you need to consider why some shares have a low PE whereas others have a high PE. The answer is that, on the whole, investors are a savvy bunch and cheap shares with low PEs are cheap for a reason whereas expensive shares with high PEs are also expensive for a reason.

Published PEs are based on past earnings data, which is usually compiled only at the end of an accounting period (usually every six months). As I've pointed out previously, investors price a share more on future earnings potential than past earnings, and often drive a share price up well beyond what's a justifiable price based on past earnings. This results in a high PE for shares that have an element of 'blue sky' potential built into their share price.

To summarise the interpretation of the PE statistic:

- *No PE:* The company isn't making a profit.

- *Low PE:* Investors are disenchanted with the business. Although past earnings have been okay, investors don't see realistic prospects of earnings growth in the future—and maybe even believe earnings will fall.

- *High PE:* This could be because the company is a solid one with a history of profitability that investors think will continue into the future—that is, the business is in the blue-chip category. So investors are prepared to pay a premium for the shares. The PE could also be high because investors realise that the business isn't very profitable at present but think there's some 'blue sky' potential for profit growth in the future.

- *Very high PE:* Usually a PE is way above average because the share price is based primarily on future profit prospects. Many speculative-type shares fall into this category.

The risk attached to buying a share with a low or high PE is also shown in figure 8.2 (overleaf).

Tip

I suggest you consider a PE of around 20 as reasonable at the present time for shares in your core portfolio.

Future profitability

Future profitability is hard to predict and always uncertain. If analysts' forecasts are available, they might help you but, in the end, you need to use your own judgement. Naturally, the further into the future you go, the greater the uncertainty—and so the lower your confidence should be in the forecast. This relationship is shown in figure 8.3.

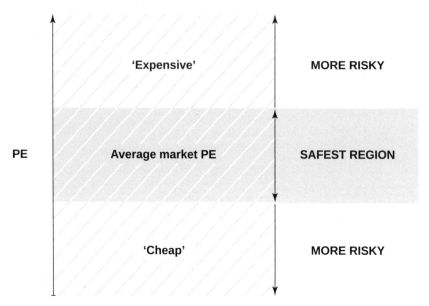

Figure 8.2: Choosing a share with a higher or lower PE than the market average increases your risk.

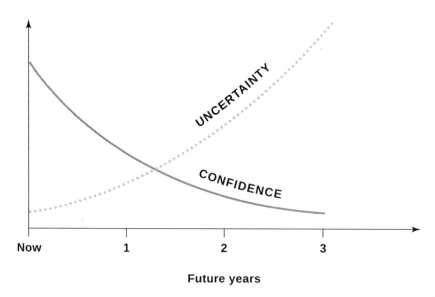

Future years

Figure 8.3: Uncertainty increases as profit forecasts get further into the future—and confidence reduces.

> **Tip**
>
> When a worldwide event such as the COVID-19 pandemic causes earnings downgrades for almost all shares, you shouldn't be too concerned about earnings downgrades for a specific share—because they occurred for virtually all shares.

Dividend statistics

In chapter 3, I explain how you can relate the dividend to the share price by a statistic known as the *dividend yield*, or just the *yield*. The yield is virtually equivalent to interest on the value of your shares. I also explain how some dividends are franked, and that the maximum level of franking is 100% or fully franked (ff). Finally, I explain how you can compare franked and unfranked dividends by using a grossing-up factor.

> **Tip**
>
> At this point, you may want to review dividend statistics—outlined in chapter 3—especially if you value dividends.

Other financial stats

Many financial stats are available that I haven't mentioned, such as those relating to the level of debt and the assets and liabilities. These can be worth consideration because companies with very high debt levels are vulnerable should there be a downturn in profitability. However, I suggest you don't try to get your head around too many statistics at this stage. Instead, concentrate on the main two I have focused on and consider really essential—namely, profit (or earnings) and dividend. These two stats, along with the general fundamentals of a company, will give you a good picture of the shares you may be considering for your core portfolio.

> **Tip**
>
> If you want to delve deeper into fundamental analysis and financial statistics, refer to either *Teach Yourself about Shares*, 3rd edition, or *Online Investing on the Australian Sharemarket*, 5th edition, both written by me and published by Wiley Australia.

Obtaining the info you need

You have two main sources for the info you need for your fundamental analysis:

- internet search
- your broker.

Internet search

A good starting point when looking for information about a company is an internet search using the company name in a search engine such as Google. For example, if you type 'BHP' or 'Goodman' in to your preferred search engine, you can quickly find the home page for each company's website. Here, you can access links to lots of info about these businesses.

The home page on a company's website will usually include an 'About us' tab or maybe 'Our business' (or some similar label) where you can obtain further details about the company. A 'Shareholders' or similar tab may also be offered, which will give you more details about the company's shares. Finally, a 'Contact us' tab will usually be included on the home page, which provides details for how to email or phone the company. I've found using the 'Contact us' facility is usually productive because I've almost always received a helpful reply to my queries.

Heaps of free websites also provide general or financial information about shares. As you might imagine, the ASX site (www2.asx.com.au) provides general and financial information about all the shares listed with the ASX so it's a good starting point for info research. After going to the site, all you need to do is search using the name or code of the share you're interested in.

Another very useful site that provides this type of info is Stockcharts (stockcharts.com.au), which has a table of all ASX-listed shares. All you need to do is click on the code of the share you're interested in and heaps of useful info will come up.

Tip

Many more websites that provide useful information are given in my book *Online Investing on the Australian Sharemarket* 5th, edition.

Your broker

Your broker—either offline or online—should be able to provide the info about a company you need. However, you're unlikely to be able to obtain much info about lower market cap, more speculative types of shares and new kids on the block from either an offline or online broker.

Offline broker

Most offline brokers should have a good idea about the companies you're interested in for your core portfolio. Some of the larger brokers have a research department and may be able to provide fairly detailed data and answer any questions you may have. Some offline brokers also have a website with info you can access if you're a customer.

Online broker

The websites of all major online brokers contain heaps of information, and you can access this info if you're a customer and able to log in to the site.

As well as info about a share, the site should provide market data so you can see how the market overall is performing. The site might also include a section titled 'Movers and Shakers' or similar that highlights shares of most interest with a high volume of trades on the day. Some of the smaller, discount-type online brokers may provide a trading service only and the website may contain very little useful data.

Tip

I suggest you don't chase the cheapest broker but be registered as a customer with at least one of the major online brokers so you can access the available info. If you're using an offline broker, nothing is stopping you also becoming a customer with an online broker—even if only to access the useful info on the site.

Let's look at the CommSec site as an example, because they're the most popular online broking site in Australia. The details I provide about this site are current at the time of writing but may change in the future—most online sites (including CommSec) periodically revise their sites, and the info provided and the way it's presented can change.

Once you've logged in to the CommSec site, you can click on the 'Quotes and Research' tab and get the latest market intel. You can then click on the 'Search' tab and enter the name or code of the share you're interested in. This takes you to a page where you'll be able to see the latest market trading data for the share, such as last price, and bids and offers. Below this are two very good charts showing historical EPS and ROE and, below these charts, are heaps of historical financial stats. This page also offers other tabs, including:

- *Summary:* Outlines current buyers and sellers and provides a chart of the share price.

- *Announcements:* Covers company announcements.

- *Charts:* Provides share price charts you can customise (more on this in the next chapter).

- *Dividends:* Includes past and current dividend data (with a bar chart).

- *Recommendations:* Outlines analyst research and findings.

- *About:* Provides a very useful snapshot of the company.

- *Forecasts and trends:* Tracks trends in earnings and earnings surprises.

- *Trade history:* Provides a summary of past trading data.

- *Financials:* Outlines past financial data.

- *Derivatives:* Provides details on warrants and options (don't worry about these derivatives because they're only for advanced traders).

So you can access heaps of info, and this is one reason I'm keen on using online brokers.

Tip

Different online broking sites have different info presented in different ways. Later on in your share investing journey, you might want to consider being a customer with more than one online broker so you can suss out several sites to find the one you prefer, or access different kinds of information as needed.

Key takeaways

- It's a really good idea to research the general and financial details about a company before you purchase its shares.

- General details cover the basic info about a company, such as how big (or small) it is, how long it's been in operation and what it actually produces and sells.

- A company has one or more products it sells to customers and so obtains sales revenue.

- Products can be of two basic types: a physical product (such as whitegoods or cars), or a service type of product (such as air transport, retailing or banking).

- A way of getting a handle on the basics of a company is by completing a SWOT analysis—where you consider the strengths, weaknesses, opportunities and threats.

- The financial details are the accounting aspects of a company. You can look at heaps of these, but the one of greatest importance is the profitability of the business.

- If a company can't make a profit, it can't last long unless it gets government support or the shareholders are prepared to prop it up.

- A company has operating costs of various types—also known as *expenses*.

- The profit a company makes is also known as *earnings*. A company operates at a profit when the revenue is greater than the expenses—otherwise, the company operates at a loss.

- For shareholders, the earnings per share (EPS) is more important than total earnings. The EPS is the earnings attributable to each issued share and is the total earnings divided by the number of issued shares.

- The EPS allows you to compare earnings of both large and small companies on an apples-to-apples basis.

- The earnings trend is of great importance, and shareholders love to see a rising EPS or at least a stable one. A falling EPS is bad news and profit downgrades are usually punished by a big drop in the share price.

- A way of getting a picture of the efficiency of a company is by the return on capital invested (ROC) or by the return on equity (ROE). Ideally, these should be above 10% and increasing, or at least remaining relatively constant.

- You can get an idea of how 'cheap' or 'expensive' a share is from the price to earnings ratio (PE), which is the share price divided by EPS. The higher the PE, the more 'expensive' the share.

- A PE that's not quoted indicates a company operating at a loss (because negative PEs aren't quoted).

- A PE of around 20 is a good benchmark value for core portfolio shares.

- A high PE can indicate a stable, profitable business that shareholders are prepared to pay a premium for. A high (or very high) PE can also indicate 'blue sky potential', with a high share price driven by market optimism.

- The sharemarket is forward looking and future earnings are more important than current or past earnings.

- For a core portfolio, I suggest you consider shares that pay a dividend. The value of the dividend is measured by the yield—which is the dividend per share divided by the share price.

- You can obtain info about the general and financial details of a company from an internet search or from your broker.

- Most of the larger online brokers have heaps of info on their website, but to access it, you need to be a customer.

Chapter 9

Getting your timing right

You should now have a good idea of how to evaluate the basic and financial fundamentals of a company and its shares. In this chapter, I consider the question of when is the best time to buy or sell shares. The answer to this question is that the most useful way to time your trades is by *charting*—that is, using charts to decide if or when you should buy or sell shares. But before we start, I've a confession to make. The title of this chapter is really a misnomer, because it's virtually impossible to get your timing exactly right. It's impossible to say whether a share price has reached a peak or trough until some time after the event, which doesn't help you at the time you're contemplating hitting the 'buy' or 'sell' button.

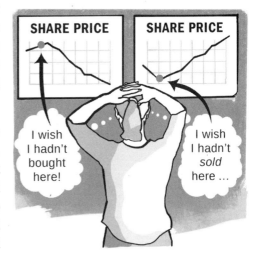

Getting your timing right may be an elusive aim, but all is not lost. Far from it! Even though you can't expect to have perfect timing and buy at the bottom and sell at the top (which is what every trader would like to do), you can aim for good timing—and that is more about avoiding disasters. These occur when you buy shares you reckon are going to be all right only to see them dive soon after, or when you sell shares you're disenchanted with only to watch them rise soon after and leave you ruing the profit you could have made if only you'd waited a while. So your aim is not to be sure all the time, but to be less unsure most of the time.

> **Tip**
>
> If you lose no more than 10% on a trade or miss out on no more than 10% potential profit, you're doing great!

Using charting to guide your trading decisions

With shares and timing your trading decisions, the most useful chart is the *price chart*, which shows how the share price has changed with time. You can also chart an index or sector using the appropriate index or sector code. For example, if you chart All Ords (XAO), you'll be able to see how the market overall has moved over the time period.

When I first started share investing in the 1970s, I had to draw share charts myself. I used big sheets of graph paper and every few days I'd check price listings and place a dot on the paper. As time went on, I joined the dots and voilà—a price chart! Nowadays, you don't have to go to all this trouble because the internet has revolutionised charting. All you have to do is call up the chart you want on your internet-connected device and bingo, up it comes! In many cases, you may even be able to customise the chart according to your preferences. Some sites allow you to access much of this wonderful technology at no cost, but other sites may require you to be a paying customer.

> ## Tip
>
> Some sites offer what they claim to be super-duper charting programs that you can subscribe to at great cost. I suggest you avoid these options because heaps of great charting programs are available for free or for low cost. After you've read and digested this chapter, you should be able to interpret charts very well and make good decisions without subscribing to some expensive service.

Obtaining the charts

You can get price charts from two main sources:

1. the internet

2. your broker.

Accessing charts online

The internet is a great place to start when looking for share charts. If you search using 'share price charts' or 'stock charts' or some similar phrase, you'll come up with lots of sites. Here are just three examples of good sites:

1. *ASX:* In addition to the fundamental info you can access from a share search on this site, there's also a useful charting facility. You can customise the chart in many ways, such as varying the time period and showing moving averages so this site is well worth a visit for basic charting — go to www2.asx.com.au.

2. *Big Charts:* This is a very popular US site where you can also access charts for Australian shares. Australian-listed shares are designated with an 'AU:' before the ASX code. The site is a comprehensive, free site with heaps of advanced features (although you don't need to access most of these at this stage). You can customise the charts in various ways and save your preferences for the next time you access the site. The chart size can be changed — I use the 'big' chart size because this is the largest and easiest to read. Some most useful info is also provided at the top of the chart, such as the PE, yield and 52-week price range. Go to bigcharts.marketwatch.com.

3. *Incredible Charts:* This is an Australian site which, like Big Charts, is a more complex site with heaps of features that you won't need to use unless you really get into charting. To access this site you need to register and download the software. Although the site used to be free, this changed in mid-2021 and now the free version is 30-day delayed, which isn't much help. However, the cost of becoming a subscriber is very reasonable — at the time of writing, only about $10 per month. You can check it out at incrediblecharts.com.

Tip

When accessing charts, computers are better than mobile phones or tablets because the screen size is much larger and it's easier to analyse the chart. You can bookmark the website on your computer so you can access the site easily.

Your broker

If you're using an offline broker, getting price charts could be a bit tricky unless the broker has a website with a charting facility. With an online broker, charting is no problem because to my knowledge all online brokers (apart from the 'trade only' ones) have a charting facility included in their website. You should be able to customise the charts in several ways and access some indicators (more on indicators later).

Tip

One of the ways online broking sites differ from each other is in their charting facilities. Checking out several of them and seeing if you prefer one over another is worthwhile. I've found the CommSec site is okay for basic charting. However, I prefer to use a dedicated charting site when contemplating a trade.

Types of price chart

Although several types of price chart are available, the main ones are:

- line chart

- OHLC chart

- candle chart

- percent chart.

Line chart

A *line chart* basically uses the same method I used when I drew my own charts. A dot marks each closing price and the dots are joined with a line. Figure 9.1 shows an example line chart.

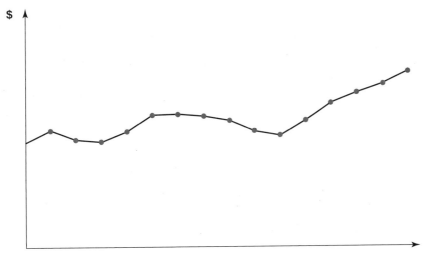

Figure 9.1: An example line chart

Sometimes the area under the line is shaded to make the line stand out more, and these variants are known as *area* or *mountain* charts.

OHLC chart

In chapter 1, I describe the four share prices of interest each day: opening, closing, high and low. Line charts have the advantage of being simple and easy to read but have the disadvantage of showing just one price—the closing price. An *OHLC chart* makes up for this shortcoming by showing all four prices. A vertical line is drawn for each day, with the bottom of the line showing the low price and the top of the line the high price. The opening price is shown by a small bar on the left of the line and the closing price by a small line to the right. Sometimes these bars are coloured for clarity. This chart appears as a series of bars from left to right across the charting space, as shown in figure 9.2.

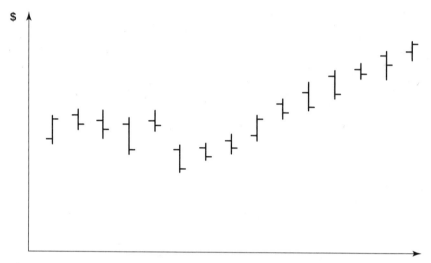

Figure 9.2: An example OHLC chart

Candle chart

A *candle chart* uses the same basic format as the OHLC chart, but instead of showing small bars on the left and right of the vertical line, a thicker bar is superimposed on the line. This looks like a candle—hence, the name of the chart. So you can tell whether the price has risen or fallen on the day, the candle is coloured. For example, for an up day, the candle may be white or green and, for a down day, the candle may be black or red. Figure 9.3 shows an example candle chart.

As you might imagine, heaps of different price scenarios with different looking candles are possible. Some possible candles are shown in figure 9.4. I'll leave it up to you to interpret the daily action depicted by each one.

Figure 9.3: An example candle chart

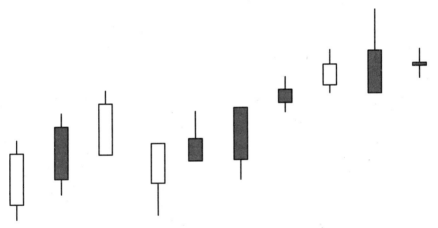

Figure 9.4: Different price scenarios produce different candles

Percent chart

A *percent chart* is a special type of chart that doesn't show prices in dollars but rather price changes as a percentage from a zero value at the start of the chart. This allows you to see the percentage rise or fall of the share price from the start point. You can make the start point the date you purchased the shares so you're able to see at a glance your percentage capital gain or loss as time unfolds.

However, the percent chart is more useful when you want to compare relative price performance. For example, suppose you want to compare Coles (COL) and Woolworths (WOW). You can call up a Coles percent chart and then use a 'compare' tab or similar to show Woolworths on this chart. Figure 9.5 shows this comparison percent chart for Coles and Woolworths, at the time of writing.

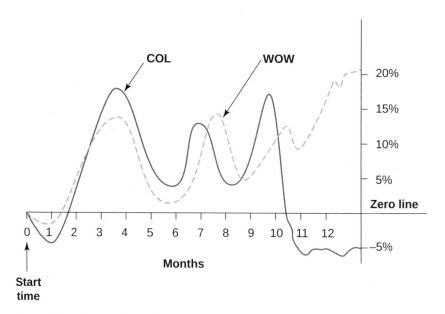

Figure 9.5: Comparing relative price performance using a percent chart

In figure 9.5, COL is the full line and WOW is the dashed line. You can see at a glance that both shares were roughly in step for the first eight months or so but after that Woolies shares started rising whereas Coles shares started falling. At the end of the time shown in the chart, Woolies shares were showing a capital gain of about 20% whereas Coles shares were showing a loss of about 5%.

Because you can also chart indices using their three-letter code, the percent chart is also useful when you want to see how a share price is performing relative to an index.

Tip

The percent chart can be useful but don't worry too much about it at this stage. You may decide to use it when you get more experienced with charting.

Choosing the time period and time interval for charting

The time period of the chart is usually a default value of one year. Usually the default time interval is one day, meaning that daily prices are shown. Depending on the charting software available, you may be able to change these and customise the chart to suit your preferences. For example, if the chart is for a long time period of several years or more, showing daily prices will create too many points or lines so you're better off with a weekly time interval.

In table 9.1, I provide my suggestions for matching time periods, time intervals and chart type, based on the purpose for your charting.

Table 9.1: Suggested combinations of time periods, time intervals, type and purpose for charting

Time period	Time interval	Chart type	Purpose
5 or more years	Weekly	Line	Long-term investing
1–3 years	Weekly or daily	Line or OHLC	Long- to medium-term investing
6 months	Daily	OHLC or candle	Medium-term or shorter term investing
1 month	Daily	Candle	Short-term investing or trading
1 day	10–15 minutes	Line	Checking price movements before placing an order

Tip

I tend to favour the candle chart format for most of my charts but if this chart is drawn over longer time periods, the candles tend to merge and this makes interpretation difficult. For a longer time period, a line or OHLC chart can be better.

Identifying trends

'Let's be friends.'

Share prices moving in some general direction is known as a *trend*. The main purpose of charting is to identify trends. The importance of trends is expressed in the well-known saying, 'The trend is your friend'.

That's to say, the percentage play is to go with the trend rather than to go against it. In the long run, you'll be better off following rather than trying to buck the trend.

Following the trend is rather like obtaining weather forecasts. Weather forecasts aren't always correct, and you can embrace them or ignore them. However, if you take an umbrella with you every time rain is forecast, you may carry it around without opening it a few times but in the long run you're far less likely to get wet.

Tip

Traders who trade against the trend are known as *contrarians*. Sometimes this tactic may pay off, but I suggest you avoid doing this unless you have very special reasons.

Types of trend

Despite all the complexity and mumbo-jumbo that chartists use, there are really only three basic trends. They are:

- *Sidetrend:* The share price tracks sideways.

- *Uptrend:* The share price trends up.

- *Downtrend:* The share price trends down.

These three basic trends are shown in figure 9.6.

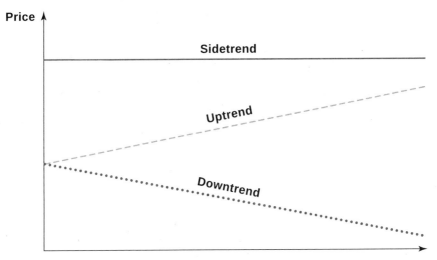

Figure 9.6: The three basic trends: sidetrend, uptrend and downtrend

Combined trends

As you might imagine, in a share price chart you'll seldom (never) see only one of these basic trends. You're far more likely to find a combination of them and this makes the longer term trend more difficult to identify. Heaps of combinations are possible, and the longer the time period of the chart, the more variations you're likely to see before one or more longer term trends emerge. In figure 9.7 (overleaf), I show just one possible combination of basic trends that form a longer term uptrend.

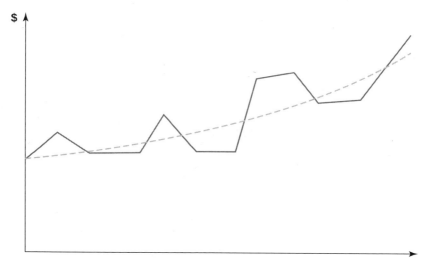

Figure 9.7: Combined trends form a longer term uptrend (dashed line)

Tip

A trend is usually shown as a straight line but the trend line can also be curved. In fact, a trend line is more likely to be curved than straight.

Identifying trends

If share prices moved in nice straight lines all the time (as shown in figure 9.6), trend identification would be dead easy and you could

make heaps of profit by buying and selling at the right time. However, real life isn't that simple. Underlying trends are masked by *noise* or *scatter*, which are the up and down variations in price each day as buyers and sellers compete.

You can think of these ups and downs as similar to being in a four-wheel-drive vehicle in the outback. You might be going up a hill, but there'll be lots of up and down movements as the car follows the terrain. So even though you're generally going in an upward direction, you won't necessarily be going up all the time; many times you might actually be going down. This scatter can make the underlying trend far more difficult to identify.

You can try to identify trends on a chart using two main methods:

- chart inspection ('eye method')

- a moving average.

Chart inspection or 'eye method'

This 'eye method' is easiest when you use a line chart, as you can see in the example shown in figure 9.8.

Figure 9.8: 'Eye method' of spotting a trend

In this case, you can spot the initial overall uptrend, which peaks and then changes to a downtrend. If you're using an OHLC or candle chart, spotting this overall trend is more difficult because now you have bars rather than points to look at. In this case, here are some simple rules for spotting the main trends:

- *Uptrend:* A line of best fit through the low points that slopes upward.

- *Downtrend:* A line of best fit through the high points that slopes downward.

- *Sidetrend:* The high and low points should be about parallel and horizontal.

These variations are shown in figure 9.9.

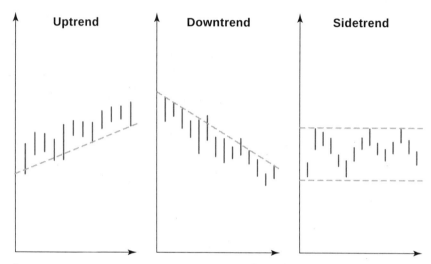

Figure 9.9: Spotting trend variations in OHLC or candle charts

Tip

Often, where you locate the trend line is rather a matter of personal judgement. Sometimes a few bars may be outside the line or cross it. The general rule is that your trend line should touch at least three bars.

Moving average method

The moving average is an aid you can use to help you to identify trends and trend changes. To see how it works, consider this example. Suppose you wanted to know if the weight of adults in a certain area was changing as time went on. To find out, you'd need to take a representative sample of adults, weigh each one and calculate the average weight of your sample. (If your maths is a little rusty, the average is obtained by adding everyone's weight and dividing by the number of people in the sample.) You would then need to repeat the experiment at a later point in time and see if the average weight had changed. You can use essentially the same idea with share prices to see how the average price of a share over a period of time was changing.

> **Tip**
>
> You don't need to worry about the details of how to calculate moving average. Your charting software will do this for you.

Several different types of moving average are possible, including:

- simple moving average (SMA)

- exponential moving average (EMA)

- weighted moving average (WMA).

The SMA is calculated just as I've described in the weight tracking example; the EMA and WMA use a different calculation where more recent prices are given more weight than the older ones. This makes the average more sensitive to recent prices than earlier ones.

> **Tip**
>
> Although the various types of moving averages are calculated differently, in practice I've found that they will all lead you to the same conclusion. If you have a choice, I suggest you use the EMA but the SMA is also fine.

INTERPRETING THE MOVING AVERAGE

The beauty of a moving average is that it smooths out the scatter on a price chart so you can identify the underlying trend more clearly. In an uptrend, the moving average line will be rising; in a downtrend, it will be falling; and in a sidetrend, it will be roughly horizontal. The disadvantage of a moving average is that the moving average takes time to respond to a trend change. For example, a 20-day SMA shows the average price 10 days ago—that is, in the middle of the past 20-day period.

TIME PERIOD

The general rule is that the shorter the time period of the moving average, the less smoothing it provides but the more sensitive the average is to trend changes. On the other hand, a longer time period provides better smoothing but reduces the sensitivity—that is, the moving average will take longer to respond to a trend change.

Some variations of this sensitivity–smoothing trade-off are shown in table 9.2.

Table 9.2: Sensitivity, smoothing and application for different moving average time periods

Time period	Sensitivity	Smoothing	Application
5–11 days	High	Low	Short-term trading
13–31 days	Medium	Medium	Medium-term trading
50 days and longer	Low	Medium–high	Longer term investing

I've also shown the differences in sensitivity and smoothness between short- and long-term moving averages in figure 9.10.

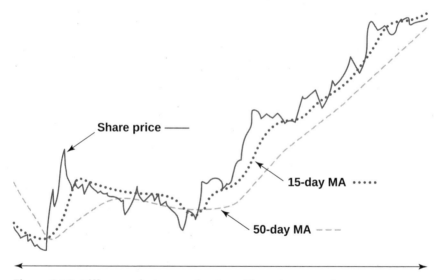

Figure 9.10: Difference between short- and long-term moving averages

Tip

You should use table 9.2 for guidance only. Charting software usually allows you to vary the time period of the moving average so you can experiment for yourself.

Trend trading

Now you know how to identify trends and trend changes, you can use this knowledge to guide your share trading decisions. The strategy that I suggest you use is a very important one, so I've added it to the six Golden Rules I outlined in chapter 5:

Golden Rule 7: Buy shares only when the price is in an uptrend and sell them only when the price is in a downtrend.

Another (and sometimes just as useful) way of expressing this rule is:

Don't buy shares when the price is in a downtrend and don't sell them when the price is in an uptrend.

Using this strategy, you can use a moving average to identify buy and sell regions, as shown in figure 9.11.

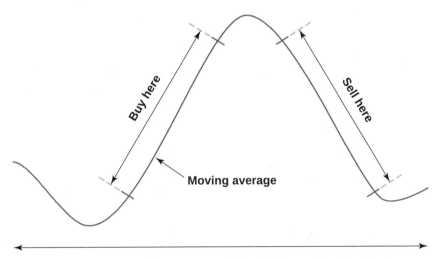

Figure 9.11: Using a moving average to identify buy and sell regions

It's very important to note that you don't aim to buy at the very lowest price but later on when the price has risen from the low. Also, you don't sell at the very highest price but at some later time when the price has fallen from the high. Naturally, you would maximise profit by buying right at the bottom of a price trend change and selling right at the top. The problem with trying to do this is that it's virtually impossible to pick the top and bottom of a trend change in real time. I believe being more confident of a trend change (and losing a little potential profit or incurring a little more loss) is better than trying to pick the top or bottom exactly and ending up making a trading decision that turns out to be wrong.

Tip

If the only thing you ever remember after reading this book is Golden Rule 7 and if you apply this to all your share trades, you'll be rewarded in spades!

More advanced charting features

There are three more advanced charting features that you want to consider, namely:

1. multiple moving averages

2. volume

3. indictors.

Multiple moving averages

Some charting software allows you to draw two or more moving averages on the same price chart. This is a worthwhile refinement, because you can see the shorter term price trends as well as the longer term ones. At times, the shorter term average may cross over the longer term one and these crossovers are usually significant because they provide trading signals. The buy signal is known as a *golden cross* and the sell signal a *dead cross*—for obvious reasons. These signals are shown in figure 9.12.

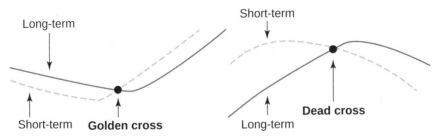

Figure 9.12: Using moving average crossover signals to identify buy and sell points

> ## Tip
>
> Obtaining two or more different time period moving averages on the same chart is well worth doing because you may be able to spot golden or dead crosses. These trading signals are usually reliable and worth acting on.

Volume

When you call up a price chart, you'll often find a smaller bar chart provided below the price chart. This bar chart shows trade *volume*. At this stage, I suggest you don't worry about trade volume other than to keep in mind the general rule that low volume price moves aren't as significant as high volume ones.

Indicators

Indicators are additional tools that help you to obtain trading signals from a chart. Heaps of different indicators have been invented—some long ago and some more recently. Each is claimed by their inventor to have some great benefit in providing a reliable trading signal.

I've tried quite a few and I haven't really found any that reliably live up to the claimed benefit, so I suggest at this stage you don't try to include any in your charting analysis. Perhaps later on if you feel more confident about charting and want to delve deeper, you could check out some of the more popular ones.

Tip

One of the problems with using indicators is that sometimes one indicator may indicate a buy signal while another indicates a sell signal. Of course, this is confusing and one reason I suggest you stick to trend identification using the 'eye method' in conjunction with one or more moving averages. Remember my general principle that erring on the side of simplicity is better than getting cluttered up in complexity.

Key takeaways

- Share price charts are very useful in helping you identify price trends, trend changes and buy and sell signals.

- You can also chart an index and this enables you to identify market or sector trends.

- Several types of price chart are available; the most common ones are line charts, OHLC charts and candle charts. Charting software often allows you to change the default type to one of the others.

- Another type of chart you may be able to obtain is the percent chart, which doesn't show prices in dollars but rather the percentage change in price from the chosen starting point. This is particularly useful if you can call up two or more lines on the percent chart because this allows you to compare the performance of a share to an index or to another share.

- The time period over which the chart is drawn can vary from very short (daily) all the way through to very long (all data). You'll usually be able to customise the time period.

- Long time period charts allow you to detect long-term trends, whereas shorter term charts are useful for detecting more recent trends. A daily chart (intra-day chart) is useful on the day you're contemplating placing an order.

- You may be able to identify a trend or trend change by inspection ('eye method'). This is easiest with a line chart but a little more difficult with a bar-type chart.

- Trends tend to be masked by price scatter or noise. One way of cutting through this noise is by using a moving average. This provides a smoothed price line. The disadvantage is that a moving average doesn't respond immediately to trend changes.

- Charting software often allows you to vary the term of the moving average. Short-term moving averages are more sensitive to trend changes but don't provide as much smoothing, whereas longer term moving averages are less sensitive to price scatter but help you to better identify underlying longer term trends and trend changes.

- A really important rule of share investing is to buy only in an uptrend and sell only in a downtrend.

- To be more certain of a trend change, you should wait a while and not try to buy at the very bottom or sell at the very top. This will reduce your profit a bit but help you to avoid wrong decisions.

- Many charting packages allow you to draw two or more moving averages on a chart. If you use a short-term moving average and a longer term one, you'll be able to detect shorter and longer term trends at the same time.

- If two different time period moving averages cross one another, the crossover points can provide good trading signals. The most important of these are the *golden cross* (buy signal) and *dead cross* (sell signal).

- Trade volumes are usually shown as a bar chart below the price chart. Price movements on small volumes are usually less significant than price moves on large volumes.

- Depending on your charting software, you can call up heaps of different indicators. However, I suggest you don't get bogged down in complexity at this stage.

Chapter 10

Buying and selling shares

By now you should have an account set up with a broker (offline or online) so you can trade shares when you want to. You know how to obtain the general details of companies you're considering investing in, including the stability of the company and its future prospects. You should also be able to look up the important financial statistics so you can check the profitability of the company and the dividend payout to shareholders. Finally, you should be able to check the timing of an order so you don't buy in a downtrend or sell in an uptrend. If the shares pass these examinations, and you want to go ahead and trade them, I'll now show you how to do so.

'Congrats! You pass my examination. Now you can join my group.'

I'll outline the nuts and bolts of trading—that is, how to trade shares, the various types of order you can place, how to develop a trading plan and the precautions you need to take before and after placing an order.

Getting down to the nuts and bolts of trading

In this section, I explain some of the basic elements of buying and selling shares, including parcel value, bids and offers, liquidity and spread.

Parcel value

You don't buy or sell shares one by one but in a *parcel*. The value of a parcel is obtained by multiplying the share price by the number of shares involved. For example, if you want to buy 2000 shares and their current price is $2.50, the parcel value is about $5000. You can also work back the other way—for example, if you have $4000 to spend and the share price is $2.00, it's easy to work out that you can buy about 2000 shares. I use the word *about* because share prices can sometimes change quickly and, even though it's usually small compared to the value of the shares, you also need to take into account brokerage.

Tip

Your broker (online or offline) will give you an estimated parcel value (including brokerage) of your order. For purchase orders, you need to ensure that sufficient cash is in an account accessible to your broker to cover the parcel value including the brokerage at the time of settlement.

Number of shares to trade

The number of shares involved in a trade is also known as the *volume* or *quantity*. Getting the number of shares you're trading exactly right is important because mistakes can be costly. You can make an error when stating the number of shares you want to buy but you can check this easily by making sure the estimated parcel value is correct.

Getting the quantity right with sell orders is also very important because you can't sell more shares than you own. Usually, your broker will check this but not always. The more common problem comes when you place a sell order for fewer shares than you own. The order will go through no problem but you're left with a small number of shares. If you've joined the dividend reinvestment plan (DRP) and want to sell all your shares, you need to be particularly careful. If you place a sell order after the shares go ex-dividend and before the allocation date, getting the quantity wrong is particularly easy. Your records will show that you own fewer shares than you're actually entitled to and, after the order transacts, you'll be allocated a small number of shares.

Tip

Try to avoid getting left with a small number of shares after your sell order transacts because these shares could be a nuisance—it might cost you more to sell them than what they're worth. There's no point holding a small number of shares and just clogging up your portfolio.

Bids and offers

A purchase order is called a *bid* whereas a sell order is an *offer*. In the course of a normal day's trading, you'll find many bids and offers for most shares. Naturally, buyers try to purchase at the lowest price they need to pay whereas sellers try to sell at the highest price they can get. As a general rule, bids and offers too far away from the action are unlikely to transact unless a dramatic trend change occurs.

Tip

In everyday speak, we often use the word 'offer' as a bid. For example, if you want to buy an item for sale, you might haggle with the seller and say something like, 'I'll offer you $x for this item'. However, with share trading, 'offer' is always used for a seller's price.

Trade price

A trade can take place only if a buyer and a seller agree on price. When a transaction occurs, the trade price becomes the market price at that time. If a buyer raises the bid from the last sale price in order to buy, the market price rises; if a seller drops the offer, the price falls. As I explain in chapter 2, price changes depend on the balance between buyers and sellers. If the volume of bids is higher than the volume of offers at close to the last sale price, the price will rise, whereas if the volume of offers is higher, the price will fall.

Tip

The way the price moves depends on *volume* rather than the number of bids and offers in the system. Some traders may want to trade many shares whereas others may want to trade only a small number.

Liquidity and spread

I explain liquidity in chapter 6, so head back there if you need to refresh your understanding.

Spread is the difference between the highest bid and the lowest offer. For example, if the highest bid is $1.19 and the lowest offer is $1.21, the spread is 2¢ ($1.21 – $1.19). This example is also shown in figure 10.1.

Figure 10.1: Spread is the difference between the highest bid and lowest offer

Tip

Liquidity and spread are closely related. The spread is usually low for liquid shares and high for illiquid ones.

Trading times

Normal trading takes place on the ASX between 10 am and 4 pm on business days. Nowadays, mobile devices make it easy for you to contact your broker at odd times. While your broker may accept orders at these times, the orders won't transact when the market is closed.

Tip

I suggest you avoid the temptation of sending orders to your broker during times when the market is closed. Also avoid the opening and closing jostling and don't place orders in the first hour or so of the market opening, or within 10 to 15 minutes of closing time.

Types of order

You can place two basic types of order—namely, buy (or purchase) orders and sell orders. Within these two basic types, most brokers (both offline and online) offer a number of variations on the theme. Three main options are possible:

- limit order
- market order
- deferred execution order.

Therefore, you may actually want to use five types of order:

- Limit buy order

- Limit sell order

- Market buy order

- Market sell order

- Stop loss sell order

Limit buy and sell orders

As the name suggests, when you place a *limit buy order* you state a price limit. This is the highest price you're prepared to pay for a certain number of shares.

In a *limit sell order*, you state a price limit at which you'll sell a certain number of shares. It's the lowest price you're prepared to accept for these shares.

Most brokers won't accept limit orders if your price limit is too far away from the last sale price. For example, if the last sale price was $2.00, you might specify a buy price limit of $1.95 or perhaps as low as $1.90. If you were selling, you might specify a price limit of $2.05 or maybe as high as $2.10, but that would be about the extent of it.

You shouldn't specify a price limit too far away from the last sale price for another good reason. Let's say the last sale price is $2.00, so you think you'll be clever and place a buy order with a limit price of $1.75. Your reasoning is that if the price drops this low, you'll pick up the shares at a really good price. Can you see what the great danger here is?

The danger is that the only way the price can drop to $1.75 is if the share price falls substantially. If the price drops this low, sure—you'll pick up the shares at a low price. But you're also buying in a falling market! As I've pointed out before, this is a big no-no and you shouldn't do this. If you're selling, the same idea applies—if the market rises substantially, you'll be selling in a rising market! This is also a big no-no that you shouldn't be part of unless you desperately need the money.

> ## Tip
>
> Avoid the temptation of placing your price limit too far away from the current market price. Even if your broker accepts the order, it's generally not a good idea.

Market orders

You place a *market order* when you can't be bothered haggling and perhaps losing the trade for the sake of a few cents. For example, it's not unusual for liquid shares trading at around $20 to have a spread of only 2¢ or so. This is a very small amount—only 0.1% of the price. To put it in perspective, if you were buying a used car with a selling price of $10000, would you really try to haggle with the seller to try to reduce the price by $10 (which is also 0.1%)? The only time a small spread is of significance is

'I'll offer you $9990.'

when you're trading a really large number of shares, because then a small difference of a few cents in price could amount to big dollars.

> **Tip**
>
> Rather than miss a sale for the sake of a few cents, consider placing market orders.

Stop loss sell order

A *stop loss sell order* is a type of deferred execution order, so called because the order won't transact until some time in the future, and only then if additional conditions you stipulate are met. As mentioned, many types of deferred execution orders are possible, but the only one I suggest you consider at this stage is the stop loss sell order.

This order is often described as rather like an insurance policy on your shares. For example, if you insure an asset you own such as a car, you pay a premium for the protection provided but if you're involved in a prang, you'll lose only a relatively small proportion of the car's value. It's the same idea with shares and when you want to be protected from a substantial price fall. The idea is that should a fall occur and you have a stop loss order in place, you'll lose only a relatively small amount of the value of the shares.

A stop loss order is really a limit sell order with an extra refinement—which is that you also specify a trigger price that's above the limit price. The idea is that your order won't go to market (that is, it won't be *triggered*) unless the price falls to the trigger price. If the price never falls to the trigger price, your order won't activate.

Deciding on a trigger price isn't easy. If you set it too far below the market price, you'll still lose a lot by the time the order activates. On the other hand, if you set it too close to the market price, you can be stopped out (your shares will be sold) on the normal small market fluctuations that aren't really significant.

> **Tip**
>
> I suggest using 10% down (at least initially) for your trigger price is a good compromise. I've found this works as well as some of the complex methods

Let's look at an example to really understand how stop loss orders work:

Current market price: $2.00.

Trigger price: $1.80 (10% down).

Limit price: $1.75.

The interpretation of this order is:

- If the price falls to $1.80, your order will activate and your shares will be sold at $1.80 if there's a buyer at this price. If not, they'll be sold at the best price below $1.80 but at no less than $1.75. If the shares still can't be sold at $1.75, your order will be held over. If the share price keeps falling below $1.75, you can then decide if you want to place an order at a lower sell price.

- If the price never falls to $1.80, your order won't go to market and you'll still own the shares. In this case, you can either cancel the order or amend it some time later and specify new trigger and limit prices.

Tip

If you've placed a stop loss order and the share price rises but you still want to be protected from a sudden fall, you can keep revising your trigger price and limit price upward. It won't cost you anything to amend the order.

Protection provided by stop loss orders

Stop loss orders seem to be a foolproof way of protecting your shares from large losses but, in practice, this protection isn't guaranteed. Stop loss orders can be ineffective when the price drops suddenly to below your limit price before the order has time to transact. This could occur in a number of ways:

- The share price gaps downward to below your price limit. Price gaps of this type are most likely to occur between the market closing one day and opening the next day, but they can also occur during a day's trading when some unexpected bad news surfaces.

- The share price essentially 'falls off a cliff'. Dramatic falls of this nature sometimes occur after a sudden change in fortunes of the company that the market hasn't expected, such as the loss of a major customer or an unexpected profit downgrade.

The share price drops due to one or more small volume trades at a substantial discount price. For example, say a shareholder has 200 shares with a last sale price of $1.00, which they just want to get rid of. A price change of 10¢ represents 10% of the value of the shares but amounts to only $20 for 200 shares, and a price change of 20¢ is 20% but still just $40. So the seller with 200 shares or so probably wouldn't baulk at selling even at a price 20% below the current price. But the share price fall resulting from a low volume trade could trigger your stop loss.

Figure 10.2 shows some of these sudden price drops in action.

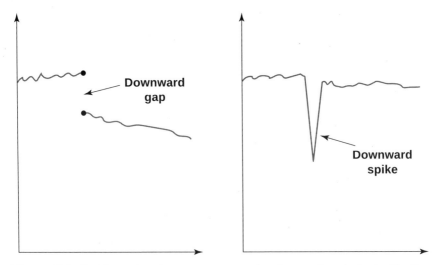

Figure 10.2: Sudden price drops can cause stop loss orders to be ineffective

Tip

You may be able to specify a minimum trade volume with your stop loss order so the order won't trigger on low volumes, but this adds a further layer of complexity.

Pros and cons of stop loss orders

Using stop loss orders does have some advantages. These include:

- A stop loss order is a 'set and forget' type of order. After you set it, you don't have to keep close tabs on the market.

- It eliminates the fear of losing (FOL) factor, where you hesitate to place a sell order on a losing share because of your aversion to taking a loss and your hope that the price might track upward again.

These orders also have some disadvantages:

- They're somewhat more fiddly to set and amend, especially if you try to build minimum volumes into your order.

- As already mentioned, they can be ineffectual during a downward gap or spike in price on a small volume of trades at a significant discount.

- The brokerage may be higher than for a plain vanilla market or limit order.

Tip

You can get the same type of protection provided by a stop loss order if you watch the market closely and place an ordinary sell order (market or limit) should the price fall to the value you would have set as your trigger price with a stop loss order.

Order duration

When you place an order, you need to specify the order duration. This is the time you'll leave your order at market if it doesn't transact quickly. When you trade liquid shares, market orders almost always transact very quickly—usually within a second or so. If you place a limit order, the order duration becomes more of an issue because the order might not transact for a long time (or maybe not at all).

I believe specifying a long order duration is not a good idea—because you don't want to buy in a falling market or sell in a rising one. If you leave an order in the system for a long time, there's a good chance this could happen.

Tip

I generally specify an order duration of just one day. If the order doesn't transact that day, I can mull over it next day in light of market movements. I can then either reactivate the same order or place a new version of it if I think it's necessary to amend any details. I certainly wouldn't specify a duration longer than about five days.

Market and share price movements

The way the shares you want to trade are trending may or may not be in step with what the market is doing at the time you're contemplating placing an order. You need to consider several possibilities, along with what these indicate for buying or selling. The ways these possibilities can combine are shown in table 10.1.

Let's look at these scenarios in a little more detail:

- *Scenario 1: Both the market and share price have the same upward direction*. This is generally a good buy indication and a poor sell indication, because you don't want to sell in a rising market.

- *Scenario 2: The market is falling but the share price is rising*. This scenario, illustrated in figure 10.3, is generally a good buy indication because it shows support for the shares is strong enough to allow them to 'buck the trend'. However, you need to exercise caution because the shares may only buck the trend temporarily but get sucked into a falling market if it's sustained.

Table 10.1: The combination of market and share price movements on buying and selling

Scenario	Market	Share price	Buy indication	Sell indication
1	Up	Up	Yes	No
2	Down	Up	Yes*	No
3	Up	Down	No*	Yes
4	Down	Down	No	Yes

*Caution should still be exercised.

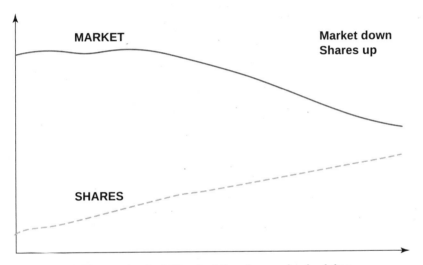

Figure 10.3: The market is falling but the share price is rising

- *Scenario 3: The market is rising but the share price is falling.* This indicates poor support for the shares and is generally a good sell indication and a poor buy indication. However, you need to exercise caution because the share price might reverse direction and the shares could be worth purchasing at some time in the future.

- *Scenario 4: Both market and share price are heading south.* This is generally a good sell indication and a poor buy indication, because you don't want to buy in a falling market.

Developing your trading plan

No doubt you know it's a good idea to have a written shopping list before shopping. Apart from eliminating the need to rely on memory, having a written list and sticking to it has another big benefit. Can you think what it is?

'I'd better check my plan before I go in.'

The benefit is that a written list helps you to avoid impulse purchases — so you avoid temptations and stick to what you really need.

A shopping list can be thought of as a trading plan for purchases. In a similar way, you need a trading plan for shares. The main difference is that a shopping list applies only to purchases, whereas you should have a share trading plan for both purchases and sales. Similar to a shopping list, however, a share trading plan helps you to avoid impulse trades based on psychological factors such as FOL (fear of loss) and FOMO (fear of missing out).

Suggested trading plan

Your trading plan could include the following:

- Name and code of the shares you intend to buy or sell.

- Expected price.

- Number of shares to be traded.

- Parcel value—which depends on the price and number of shares. You can also include expected brokerage on the trade.

- Type of order—whether a limit order, market order or deferred execution order.

- Reason—why you want to buy or sell these shares.

- Time period—how long you intend to hold purchased shares.

- Profit target—expected capital gains and dividends for purchased shares.

- Sell criteria—known as your *exit strategy*.

Tip

Having a pro-forma plan for purchases and sales is a good idea. Then you can just fill out the details for each proposed trade.

Using this suggested trading plan, a sample purchase plan could be as follows:

Name and code of shares: Acme shares (AC1).

Expected price: $1.50.

Number of shares: 2000.

Parcel value: $3020, including brokerage.

Type of order: Limit order of $1.55.

Reason: I want to buy these shares because they're a diversified exchange traded fund with a good profit record and pay good, reliable fully franked dividends.

Time period: Long term.

Profit target: 10% pa, based on 5% average price growth and 5% grossed-up dividend.

Sell criteria: An unexpected adverse change or if the price trends down by more than 10%.

A sample selling plan could be:

Name and code of shares: Zed shares (XYZ).

Expected price: $1.50.

Number of shares: 2000.

Parcel value: $3020, including brokerage.

Type of order: Market order.

Reason: I want to sell these shares because they're no longer performing as they did when I bought them. Also the dividend has been cut.

Time period: Doesn't apply to selling orders.

Profit target: Ditto.

Sell criteria: If maximum loss reaches $350.

Tip

Trading according to a plan is a really good idea, especially for purchase trades. Your purchase plan should include an exit strategy (your sell criteria) in case things go pear-shaped.

Placing orders

When placing an order, you need to concentrate, so you need a quiet environment free of distraction and interruptions. I suggest you sit down with a pencil or pen, paper, calculating device and your shares file (if you have one). Placing orders while on a golf course waiting to tee off is really not a good idea!

Tip

It might be a good idea to get yourself a coffee, tea or cold drink (non-alcoholic) so you can relax and mull over a proposed order before you actually place it.

Offline orders

If you're using an offline broker, you just need to get in touch with your broker by whatever means you've both agreed on and discuss what you have in mind. The broker will give you an order estimate and if you both agree on the details of the trade, you don't need to do any more and the broker will place the order.

Online orders

You place online orders by logging into your trading site and going to the trading section. Here, you enter the code of the shares you wish to trade. You'll then be shown a trading screen for these shares that should show the following:

- Summary of the latest price action, indicating whether the price has risen or fallen and the volume of trades so far.

- The latest trade price and the bids and offers closest to this price.

A table will usually show buy orders on the left and sell orders on the right, and these will be ranked in price order. For each bid or offer, the table shows the number of buyers or sellers and the total number of shares bid or offered at each price.

Another table is also usually shown where you can enter the details of your order, including:

- whether you're placing a buy or sell order

- the number of shares you want to trade

- your order type, such as market or limit; if a limit order, your price limit

- order duration.

If you're placing a conditional order such as a stop loss order, the trading screen will be a little different because you'll need to specify your trigger limit as well as your price limit.

Daily price movements

If you want to fine-tune your trade, you can get an idea of how the share price is likely to move on the day by looking at the volume of bids and offers at market closest to the most recent trade price. The price is most likely to rise when there's a higher volume of bids and fall when there's a higher volume of offers.

Another option is to check the trades history for the day (also known as *course of sales*). This is a list of trades that have occurred so far. If the shares are liquid, heaps of trades could have occurred after a few hours of trading, so it's easier to look at an *intra-day* chart. This is a one-day chart showing the price action up to that point in time. It usually also shows trade volume as a bar chart below the price chart. The chart may also include a moving average trend line. A typical intra-day chart is shown in figure 10.4. Note that the chart is drawn to only 2.30 pm because that's the time the data was accessed.

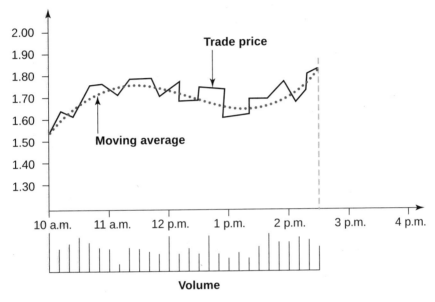

Figure 10.4: An example intra-day chart

Tip

Not all online brokers provide intra-day charts, but if you can get one, checking it is much more convenient than trying to analyse heaps of figures. If you're buying shares for your core portfolio that you expect to hold for a long time, you don't need to concern yourself too much about short-term price moves at the time you're planning your purchase.

Order estimate

After you've inserted the details of your order, you'll be given an *order estimate*. This tells you the estimated total value of your order, including brokerage. The order is only an estimate at this stage because the market can move so quickly that by the time your order goes to market, prices may already have changed.

Order confirmation

Before your order goes to market, you'll be asked for final confirmation. This is your last chance to change anything. If all details are correct, you can confirm the order; otherwise, you can cancel it. Once you confirm the order, you have no further control and your order will be sent to market.

If you're trading online, your broker should send you an email or text confirming your order and its details. In the rare chance that something is incorrect, you need to contact your broker immediately. With a market order, you won't be able to do this because the order will most likely have transacted before you have time to amend anything.

Order transaction

Once your order goes to market, it will remain there until it transacts or its time period expires. If it hasn't transacted within the time period you stipulated, it will be cancelled. A market order should transact very quickly. For a limit or deferred execution order, the time to transact depends on how the market moves and how far your price or trigger limits are from the latest sale price.

After your order transacts, you should receive confirmation from your broker and this will most likely include a contract note. If you're using an online broker, your advice should come through almost immediately in electronic form, but with an offline broker it will depend on what arrangements you've agreed on.

The contract note shows all details of the order, including:

- contract date
- code and name of the company
- number of shares traded
- trade price

- total trade value

- brokerage and possible other charges, including GST

- net cost to you for a buy order or net revenue for a sell order

- settlement date.

In some cases, your order may transact in multiple parcels, depending on whether the broker was able to finalise the transaction in one parcel. Multiple parcels will show on your contract note but won't make any difference to you, because these parcels will be amalgamated in the one contract and you won't incur additional brokerage.

Settlement

As I mention in chapter 5, settlement is T+2 meaning that financial settlement takes place two days after the contract date. The broker takes their cut, and the remaining cash is taken out of or deposited into your account, depending on whether you placed a buy or a sell order.

Tip

T+2 settlement doesn't depend on the time of day. If your order transacts early on, say, Monday morning or late in the afternoon, it's still regarded as a Monday trade and settlement will occur on Wednesday. The time of settlement on Wednesday is not set in concrete and you won't know at what time it occurred until you check your account balance.

Amending your order

The general rule is that you can amend your order any time before it transacts and you shouldn't be up for additional brokerage. For example, suppose you place a purchase order for 5000 shares at a limit price of $1.50. However, your order doesn't transact because the share price rises above your limit. A few days later, the price has risen to $1.60. You now realise that you're very unlikely to pick up the shares at $1.50 so you amend your order and stipulate a higher price. This should be no problem with no cost to you.

Suppose, however, that your broker was able to get 3000 shares at $1.50. If you really want 5000 shares, you'll need to cancel the remaining order for 2000 shares at $1.50 and place another order for 2000 shares at the higher price of around $1.60 (or a market order). This order will be regarded as a new one and if it transacts, you'll receive another contract note and you'll be up for additional brokerage.

Receiving your CHESS statement

Assuming you've joined CHESS, some time after your order transacts you'll receive a CHESS statement. You'll also receive a new CHESS statement if you didn't actually trade shares but were allocated additional shares because you joined the DRP. The CHESS statement also shows details of the share registry for the shares.

Tip

When you receive a new CHESS statement, check to ensure that the number of shares shown exactly matches your records. In the rare case of any discrepancy, you need to investigate. Perhaps your records are in error but if they seem correct and you're still fogged, you need to contact the broker or share registry to try to clear up the mystery.

Key takeaways

- You should place an order to trade shares only after you've made sure the shares conform to your criteria and you're satisfied that now is a good time to place the order.

- The parcel value is the total amount of money you'll need to fork out for a purchase or the amount you'll receive when you sell.

- The parcel value depends on the number of shares and the trade price. If you place a purchase order, you need to ensure that sufficient cash is in an account accessible to your broker to cover the parcel value and the brokerage.

- You need to be particularly careful about the number of shares you plan to trade, especially if you've joined the DRP and want to sell all your shares.

- Buyers place *bids* whereas sellers place *offers*. A trade occurs only when a bid and an offer match exactly in all details.

- *Spread* is the difference between the highest bid and lowest offer at market. It's closely related to liquidity and is usually low for liquid shares and high for illiquid shares.

- You can essentially place three types of orders—namely, limit orders, market orders and deferred execution orders.

- Many types of deferred execution orders are possible and they can get quite complex but the only one you're likely to want to use is the stop loss order.

- You place a limit order when you want to hold out for the maximum price you're prepared to pay when you're buying shares or the minimum price you want if you're selling them.

- You place a market order when you want the order to transact quickly and you don't want to haggle about a small price difference.

- You place a stop loss order when you want to protect yourself from a large price fall should it occur. However, stop loss orders aren't always effective and you can get the same protection by keeping close tabs on the market and placing an ordinary sell order if it becomes necessary.

(continued)

- You need to specify order duration, which is the amount of time you want the order to remain at market if it doesn't transact quickly.

- Specifying a long order duration is generally not a good idea because you might end up buying in a falling market or selling in a rising one.

- You should take notice of market and share price movements at the time when you wish to place an order. If they're both moving in the same direction, you have a clear signal; if they're moving in the opposite direction, you need to consider this more carefully.

- Following a trading plan when you contemplate a trade is a good idea. You need a plan for both purchases and sales.

- When planning purchases, make sure you include an exit strategy in case things go pear-shaped later on.

- When you place orders, either offline or online, you need to do so in a quiet environment free of distractions.

- You place offline orders by contacting your broker directly. You place online orders by logging onto your site and going to the trading screen, where you insert the required details.

- Make sure to check all details of your order carefully before you confirm it.

- After your order transacts, you'll receive confirmation and a contract note showing the exact amount of money involved. You'll also receive a CHESS statement later on showing the changes to your shareholding as a result of the transaction.

- You'll also receive a new CHESS statement if you receive shares through a DRP.

- You need to carefully check CHESS statements to ensure all details match your records. If you spot any discrepancies, contact your broker or the relevant share registry without delay.

Chapter 11

Managing your shares

Now you know how to set up a good portfolio of shares, it's not a matter of just sitting back and relaxing and reaping the profits. You need to manage your investment on an ongoing basis and, as I pointed out way back in chapter 1, this is the most important part of being a successful share investor. Managing your shares successfully is what I look at in this chapter.

Setting up a share portfolio is really like going into business for yourself. Every business needs to be managed on an ongoing basis, including keeping up to date and making sure the business performs to your satisfaction. If it doesn't, you need to decide what you intend to do about it.

Managing your share portfolio involves four key activities.

Four key activities

The four activities involved in managing your shares are:

- *Keeping tabs:* Known as *monitoring*.

- *Reviewing:* Deciding whether or not you're happy with the performance of your shares.

- *Decision-making:* Deciding if some action is needed.

- *Acting:* Carrying out your decision.

Keeping tabs

You want to monitor your shares for two reasons:

- To keep up to date with your shares or perhaps other shares you may be interested in.

- To complete your income tax return for the financial year.

You need to decide on how often you think you need to monitor your shares and the market. If you own any speculative shares (or are thinking of buying some), they'll be volatile — meaning the price can change fairly dramatically in the short term — so daily monitoring may be necessary.

'Now to forget about you …'

Longer term 'quality' shares don't need to be watched so closely and once a week monitoring should be adequate. With quality type shares you shouldn't pay much attention to the inevitable short-term price fluctuations, because these are a normal part of the sharemarket. In fact, an approach known as the *bottom drawer approach* is a 'set and forget' type of approach where you don't even bother to keep tabs on your quality shares. The idea is that you won't worry about the short-term fluctuations because you won't even know about them. If you have quality shares, they should perform over the longer term so why worry in the short term?

Tip

While I don't recommend an approach as drastic as the bottom drawer approach, I certainly endorse the idea of not letting small fluctuations in the price of quality shares worry you.

How to monitor

I've mentioned previously the 'good old days' when I first started getting into shares. In those days, the most common way of keeping tabs on shares was newspapers, all of which had a page or two of share price listings as well as a stockmarket report. Nowadays, better ways of keeping tabs on shares are available, but newspaper and financial journal reports can still be a useful way of keeping track of sharemarket developments and for getting ideas about shares.

If you trade offline, your broker should furnish you with a summary of the performance of your share portfolio on a regular basis. Some brokers also research shares and have reports offering company info that you should be able to access.

If you trade online, your broker should automatically set up a portfolio of the shares you own that you've purchased with the broker. You should also be able to access your trade's history. If you have a dedicated trading account with the broker, you can check the balance of the account and any upcoming payments or transactions.

Your online portfolio should be updated in real time and show the following details:

- code of each of the shares you own and the number of shares

- estimated purchase price

- last trade price

- estimated (paper) profit or loss on each shareholding

- *weighting* of each of your shares—that is, the percentage value of each of the shares in your portfolio

- total market value of your portfolio and estimated (paper) profit or loss on it.

Note: The purchase price and profit or loss totals are estimates only. These will be fairly accurate if you bought shares in only one parcel and you're not in a dividend reinvestment plan (DRP). The waters become muddy when you've bought or sold in different parcels, or you've received shares through a DRP or from other transfers. In this case, the profit or loss values shown in your online portfolio aren't accurate and certainly can't be used for tax purposes.

Using a watch list

You should be able to set up a 'watch list' with your online broker. This is a list of the shares you're interested in but you haven't purchased. The beauty of a watch list is that you can keep tabs on the shares in it with one click of a button rather than having to enter each code separately.

Completing your income tax return

At the end of each financial year, to complete your income tax return you need to include any income derived from your share activities. As discussed previously, the two sources of shares income are:

- dividends and imputation credits received during the year

- capital gain (or loss) on shares you've sold during the year.

Remember—you don't need to include the paper profit or loss with shares in your portfolio that weren't sold during the year.

If you use an income tax accountant, all you need to do is provide your dividend statements and trading contracts for the year. Your accountant will then summarise these and include them in your tax return.

If you don't use an accountant, you'll need to compile this information yourself. To do this, you need to systematically go through your shares files and total up all the dividends as well as capital gains or losses. Life is a lot easier with regard to dividends if you submit your tax return using the tax office's online myTax facility, because you can opt to have your tax return pre-filled. Your broker should have provided the ATO with your tax file number when you first set up your account so, come tax time, the tax office should have all your dividend information. You'll still have to calculate your capital gains or losses, but this shouldn't be too difficult if you've maintained a good filing system and have kept track of all your share trades.

Tip

Some brokers and share registries can compile a tax summary of your shares transactions but may charge for this service.

Reviewing

Reviewing is the process of looking at your portfolio and each of the shares in it and deciding if you're satisfied with their performance. Reviewing goes hand in hand with monitoring, because you naturally review as you monitor. For example, when you check the latest share price you might think, *Great, the price has risen* or you might think, *Oh no, the price has fallen.* In so doing, you're really reviewing performance. After you've reviewed the shares in your portfolio, you'll most likely review the shares on your watch list so as to keep up to date with their developments.

Even though monitoring and reviewing go hand in hand, they're really different activities. You have no control over what your monitoring will reveal—you're just finding out what's been going on. The market will have gone its own sweet way regardless of what you thought it would do or what you would like it to have done.

'Why aren't you going the way I want you to?'

On the other hand, when you review, you're exercising control because you can come to conclusions and decide if you want to change something.

I suggest you carry out three types of review:

- review your shares

- review your portfolio

- review your trades.

Reviewing your shares

You can review your shares as often or as seldom as you like, depending on the types of shares you're monitoring and the way the market is moving. I like to monitor and review my shares fairly thoroughly once a week—generally on a weekend when I have more time. I do this by logging into my broker's online website and also my charting website.

I check the price of each of my shares and their change in value during the week. I then look at the price chart and make sure I'm happy with the trend or any recent changes in trend. I make a brief note if I feel any action may be needed. After I've reviewed all the shares in my portfolio, I also review the shares in my watch list and decide whether now is a good time to buy.

Tip

If any unexpected gaps or sudden changes in trend occur, it's worthwhile checking if the gap was due to the shares going ex-dividend or if any company announcements could shed light on the cause. Your online broker's website should have a list of company announcements, and charting software may also provide a chart with announcements marked.

Reviewing your portfolio

Each week when I review my shares I also review the performance of my portfolio. I calculate the performance of my portfolio and then compare it to the performance of the market. I do this by working out the percentage change in value of my portfolio and the market. I use the following formula for both:

$$\% \text{ change} = \left(\frac{\text{This week's value}}{\text{Last week's value}} - 1 \right) \times 100$$

For calculating the market change, I use the All Ords index (XAO) because I consider it to be the best indicator of the Australian market. You could use any indicator you think appropriate.

Tip

The performance calculations I've included here are built into my spreadsheet so they're automatic.

Here's an example of working out this percentage change in performance. Say last week my portfolio value was \$125 416 and the XAO was sitting at 7325. This week, my portfolio value is \$126 503 and the XAO is 7378.

The percentage change for my portfolio is as follows:

$$\% \text{ change} = \left(\frac{126\,503}{125\,416} - 1\right) \times 100$$
$$= (1.0087 - 1) \times 100$$
$$= 0.0087 \times 100$$
$$= 0.87\%$$

For the market, the percentage change is:

$$\% \text{ change} = \left(\frac{7378}{7325} - 1\right) \times 100$$
$$= (1.0072 - 1) \times 100$$
$$= 0.0072 \times 100$$
$$= 0.72\%$$

This comparison shows me that my share portfolio and the market both had good gains last week, with my portfolio slightly outperforming the market, so I'm really happy!

Reviewing your trades

Reviewing your trades some time after settlement is a good idea. When you traded the shares, you should have (hopefully) been following your plan. If you did follow your plan, regardless of how the trade pans out, you should still give yourself a pat on the back—'well done'. If your trade turns out to be a loss one, try to find out why because this could help you to make better trades in the future.

'I'm happy I'm keeping pace.'

Tip

As I've said so many times before, the sharemarket can be unpredictable. So if your trade didn't work out as planned, don't beat yourself up about it—unless you made some silly error. Some of your trades will inevitably be unsuccessful; the trick is to make more profit with your successful trades than you lose with your unsuccessful ones.

If you didn't follow your plan when you made the trade, you need to be honest with yourself and try to figure why this happened. You might come up with reasons such as:

- 'I acted on impulse because I was in an optimistic (or pessimistic) mood.'

- 'I got fed up with the shares because I've held them for a long time and they hadn't performed.'

- 'I received a "hot tip" I wanted to act on before the market wised up to it.'

- 'I was too busy to do the research I should have done before acting.'

Tip

Strange to say, but research shows that weather usually has a profound impact on human moods, which in turn can affect the sharemarket. On fine, sunny days, investors usually feel optimistic and drive the market up, whereas on overcast, chilly or rainy days, the opposite is more likely. The time of the week or year (including the season) can also affect human moods and, in turn, the sharemarket.

Being honest with yourself about the reason or reasons you didn't follow your plan will help you to avoid making the same mistake in the future. And let's face it—if you don't have a trading plan or if you have one and you didn't follow it, you've made a mistake.

Tip

Very rarely will you get an edge on the market by acting quickly. The market is usually very 'au fait' with developments and responds very quickly to changes. Indeed, the market frequently responds to rumour rather than fact and reacts before the news actually eventuates.

Decision-making

As you review your portfolio performance, as well as the performance of each of the shares in it, you can decide if you're happy with the state of affairs or if you need to change anything. In other words, you need to make managerial decisions about your shares. Also, you need to look at shares you've earmarked for possible purchase and decide if now is the time to buy.

If your review indicates that you need to take some action, you need to decide what action to take. In my case, as long as my portfolio keeps pace with the market, I'm satisfied because I believe it's not realistic to expect my portfolio to outperform the market on a continuing basis. However, if my portfolio performs significantly worse than the market, I start to get concerned and I try to ascertain the reason and if I need to do anything. Naturally, I'd like all my shares to rise in value each week but again that's not a realistic expectation. If any of my shares aren't performing as I planned when I purchased them, alarm bells start to ring and I keep a closer watch on these shares so I can decide if I should do something about it.

With regard to your portfolio as a whole or each of the shares in it, you have the following choices when deciding what to do:

- *Do nothing:* If you're happy with the performance, there's no need for action.

- *Earmark shares for closer watch:* You're not happy with the performance, but you decide to defer action for the time being.

- *Re-jig your portfolio:* This will involve selling some shares you own and substituting some new ones. This will most likely include shares in your watch list.

It's up to you to decide which of these will apply. It's not an easy decision as each one has pros and cons.

Acting

This is when you put your decisions into practice. Monitoring, reviewing and making decisions is pointless if you don't actually act on the decisions you've made.

Taking action is particularly difficult when a share isn't performing and you've decided you should sell some or maybe all of them but you're reluctant to swallow the bitter pill and overcome the FOL hurdle. It's very easy to procrastinate, especially if you've done your reviewing and decision-making over the weekend (as I do)—because you can't trade until at least Monday when the market's open for trading again. When Monday rolls around, you may get involved in work or other activities and so taking action on your shares can easily be relegated to the back burner.

> **Tip**
>
> Remember and apply the Nike motto to your shares and acting on your decision-making: Just do it!

Trading frequency

When you look at a price chart over a past period for a particular share, no doubt you'll be able to identify points where you could have made lots of profit by buying and selling at just the right time.

This can lead to the conclusion that by trading frequently, you can increase your profitability considerably compared with just holding the shares after you bought them. The problem with this is that you can't trade retrospectively and you can't identify perfect buy and sell points in advance. Numerous studies over the years have demonstrated that frequent trading doesn't improve profitability—in fact, it reduces it. In other words, frequent trading is a *wealth hazard*. Indeed, an optimum level of trading is possible, as shown in figure 11.1.

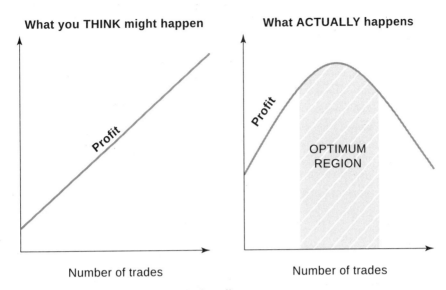

Figure 11.1: The optimum level of trading

The take out from all this is that you need to be careful not to trade too seldom and 'sit on your hands' for too long, especially when a share's price is trending down. At the same time, you need to avoid the temptation to trade too often and try to pick the highs and lows of share price fluctuations and acting on each of them. Avoid the 'grass is greener on the other side' mentality and be realistic about your trading. If you own quality shares, erring on the side of conservatism is best — don't try to sell and buy back each time there's a price rise or fall.

If you've bought some speckies, you do need to keep a closer eye on them and trade more frequently because they're far more likely to require tweaking as time goes on.

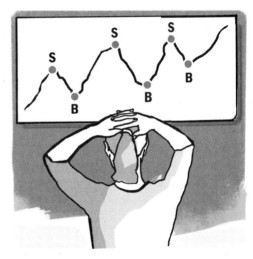

'Wow! I could have made a lot more profit if I had sold at points "S" and bought at points "B".'

Compiling and maintaining records

Record-keeping is probably the most boring part of share investing but it's really important to keep good shares records, not only for your own benefit but also to keep the tax office happy. Eventually, keeping good records will also benefit your beneficiaries, because your shares are an asset that will be included in your estate.

You can maintain records either as paper documents or as electronic files or a combination of both. Paper documents were the norm in years gone by but nowadays most companies and share registries try to persuade you to receive all your info electronically. The reasons are obvious—it's cheaper and faster and more environmentally friendly.

Tip

It's distinctly possible that in the not-so-distant future paper documents for shares will become obsolete, so you'll have to maintain all your share records electronically.

Records to keep

You need to be selective about the amount of info you'll keep about your shares, especially if you have a fairly large portfolio. I suggest you maintain the following records:

- portfolio details
- transactions
- contract notes
- shares file
- capital gains
- sold shares.

If you opt for paper documents, you need an efficient filing system with a separate file for each share in your portfolio. If you keep electronic records, make sure you back up your files on a separate storage device so your records won't be lost if some electronic malfunction occurs.

Portfolio details

I compile a portfolio spreadsheet of my own that I update each week. Here I keep details such as number of shares and their price, dividend type and yield. When I update it the old one is overwritten and lost. I print and save a copy after I've completed updating, so I have a permanent record I can refer to at any time.

'I think I need a file.'

My online broker provides an up-to-date portfolio each time I enter the site and I use this to update my own spreadsheet. The added bonus of having my own spreadsheet is that as I update it each week, my attention focuses on each of my shares. If you're not really au fait with spreadsheets and you don't want this hassle, the easier option is to download your portfolio from your broker's website and keep a copy. If you print a hard copy, you can write any reminders or notes on it—maybe using a red pen.

Tip

I provide details of my portfolio spreadsheet in the appendix, so you can see the basic format. You could use the same format or simplify it or make changes as you see fit.

Transactions

I maintain a master file of all my share transactions. I insert a space at the end of each financial year so I can easily distinguish each year's trades. I've found this file to be most useful and well worth keeping.

Contract notes

Contract notes are legal documents so keeping them on file is worthwhile. If you're using paper copies, a single file will do—in fact, you can use your transactions file with your master transactions sheet at the front and the contract notes filed in date order behind this. Of course, you can organise electronic files in a similar way.

Shares file

I maintain a file for each of the shares in my portfolio. I insert relevant information in this file so I can look back over the info later on if I want to. This includes CHESS statements, press releases, shareholder briefings and reports and results of AGMs.

I keep dividend statements for each share in the relevant file. In the front of the file, I keep a dividend summary sheet that I update each time I receive a dividend. If I've joined the DRP, I calculate and show the accounting cost of the shares I now own. This is the cost of the shares for accounting and tax purposes. When you receive a dividend and elect to take it in shares rather than cash, this changes the accounting cost of the shares you own. You could well argue that these shares were free to you but that's not how the accountants or ATO see it! They regard shares received through a DRP as if they were purchased by you at the allocation price. This changes the profit or loss and the capital gains tax if you later sell any of them.

For example, say you buy 1500 ACME shares at a cost of $3.41 each. With brokerage, the total cost of the shares is $5135. The shares are fully franked and you join the DRP. After a few months, you get your first dividend statement, which contains the following info:

- *Dividend per share:* 19¢.

- *Total dividend:* $285 (this is 1500 × $0.19).

- *Franking credits:* $85.50.

- *Shares allocation price:* $3.40.

- *Number of shares held:* 1500.

- *Number of shares allocated:* 83.

- *Cost of shares allocated:* $282.20 (this is 83 × $3.40).

- *Amount carried over:* $2.80 (this is $285 − $282.20).

- *Number of shares now held:* 1583.

You now have 1583 shares at an accounting cost of $5417.20 (which is $5135 + $ 282.20).

Note: I've shown all the details and calculations contained in your DRP dividend statement but, of course, you don't have to do any of these. Your only calculation is adding the cost of the shares allocated to your original cost. When you receive your next dividend, you again need to add the cost of the next lot of shares allocated to the previous cost of $5417.20 and so on.

Tip

You don't need to worry about cents for tax purposes and you can round off the cost of your shares to the nearest dollar.

Capital gains

As well as keeping a master transaction file, I also maintain a capital gains spreadsheet that I update each time I sell shares. At the end of a financial year, I have the up-to-date capital gains info I need to include in my tax return.

Sold shares file

If you sell all your shares, you can remove your shares file because you'll no longer need it. You should go through the documents in the file and remove the ones you want to keep and place them in a 'sold shares' file. Generally, the only documents I keep for sold shares are the CHESS statements and dividend statements. You need to keep your trading contracts but if you have followed my suggestions these will be a separate file anyway, which you should maintain indefinitely.

Key takeaways

- When you become a shareholder, you're actually a part-owner in a business and, as with any business venture, your shares need to be managed.

- To manage your shares, you need to engage in four activities: monitoring (or keeping tabs), reviewing, making decisions and taking any necessary action.

- You need to keep tabs on your shares so you can keep yourself up to date and also because it's a legal requirement that you have appropriate records of income from your shares. It's also important for your estate because your shares are an asset and will be part of it.

- When you become a client with an online or offline broker, the broker should automatically set up your portfolio, which shows the shares you own and their current value. If you use an online broker, your portfolio will be up to date in real time and you can access it anytime you like.

- You might also like to maintain your own portfolio spreadsheet so you can include additional info not shown in your broker's portfolio. It's worthwhile keeping copies of your portfolio that you can refer to later on.

- Online brokers will usually have a 'watch list' function so you can easily keep an eye on shares you're interested in but don't actually own.

- After you review and make decisions about your portfolio and the shares in it, you need to take action to put your decisions into practice. Try to avoid procrastinating (putting off difficult or painful actions) and just do it!

- With your core (quality) shares, you don't need to worry about short-term price fluctuations because these are a normal part of the sharemarket. You do need to focus on longer term trends or trend changes.

- Profit from shares is taxable income and you need to consider both dividends and capital gains profits.

- Many brokers (both offline and online) will provide an end of financial year dividend summary, and the ATO will also pre-fill these if you use the online myTax system.

- Capital gains tax income is rather more difficult to calculate because you may acquire shares at different times and costs and also receive shares through a DRP. So you need to keep accurate records of all your share transactions.

- Even if you don't use a tax accountant, compiling the necessary share income info isn't too difficult, provided you keep systematic and accurate records.

Chapter 12

Turbocharging your share investment

In previous chapters, I've outlined the basics of share investing and the terms and concepts I think you need to be aware of. I've also discussed how you can make shares a good investment. In this chapter, I now look at some strategies you can use to make your share investing even more profitable. I also alert you to some possible traps you could fall into and that you need to avoid if you really want to fly high.

The power of compounding

As you know, if you're going to be a share investor and you really want to make shares a good investment, you need to be in it for the longer term. This allows you to take advantage of what is known as the *power of compounding*. This is also known as the *magic of compounding* but, actually, nothing is magical about it because it's based on mathematics.

To tap into this power, you need to forgo instant gratification so you can obtain future benefits. When you're making a profit, spending that profit on something you'd like right now is very tempting. And let's face it, just about everyone has something they'd like right now so there's a real temptation to spend now and worry about tomorrow—well, tomorrow. However, if you're going to take advantage of compounding, you need to change this mindset. You need to think about the future and not let instant gratification overrule your longer term ambitions. If you can do this, compounding will reward you in spades.

What you have to do is simple: re-invest your profits back into your investment and not spend them. The effect of compound growth on the value of an investment is shown in figure 12.1.

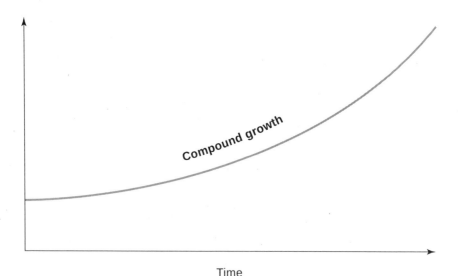

Time

Figure 12.1: The power of compound growth

Tip

The longer the time period of your investment, the greater the effect compounding has in increasing the value of the investment.

You can see from figure 12.1 that with compound growth the line showing the value of the investment isn't a straight one but curves upward. So, as time goes on, the rate of growth gets increasingly greater.

Average share growth

Now let's consider the compound growth of the Australian sharemarket over the years. The best way of doing this is by tracking the All Ords index (XAO), because it comprises 500 of the largest listed Australian companies. In 1980, the All Ords was set at a nominal benchmark value of 500 points. In 2021, after recovering from the COVID-19 induced meltdown, the All Ords had climbed up to around 7600 points.

Using a standard compound interest formula, the compound growth factor of the All Ords works out to be a little less than 6.9%. That's to say, with an annual growth rate of 6.9%, 500 would grow to about 7700 in 41 years.

Let's now look at how the annual growth rate works out over time.

Suppose you have $10 000 to invest and consider two scenarios:

- You invest in what might be regarded as a 'safe' investment growing at 3% pa.

- You invest in quality Australian shares that grow at an average rate of about 7% pa.

The compound growth in value of these investments over different time periods is shown in table 12.1.

Table 12.1: Compound growth at 3% and 7% pa

Year	3% pa growth	7% pa growth
5	11 600	14 000
10	13 400	19 700
20	18 100	38 700
30	24 300	76 100

You can see that the different growth rates don't produce huge differences in the short term. However, over the longer term, getting that extra 4% growth amounts to big dollars. The huge long-term compound growth of invested capital explains how superannuation funds can give members big payouts when they retire after contributing payments over a long working career.

The difference between 'safe' investments and shares is really much greater when you consider that interest in a 'safe account' is taxable income and tax reduces profit. This means the net return on a 3% growth rate could be as low as 2% or so. That's not the case with shares, because capital gains are payable only if you sell. Even then, most of the capital gain would qualify for the 50% discount. If by that time you've retired and no longer working, you might have to pay income tax anyway.

Tip

Gaining a few percent extra return on your investment produces a huge long-term benefit.

Effect of withdrawing profit

In the scenario just discussed, if you withdrew the capital gains profit you made each year and spent it, at the end of 10, 20 or 30 years you'd still have just $10000 worth of shares (the amount you originally invested). To make matters worse, over the years inflation kicks in and your original $10000 would be worth much less in real terms—that is, with regard to what you could purchase with the money.

Tip

Deciding between putting your money into a 'safe' investment earning low interest that's taxable income and turbocharging your investment with shares that enable you to obtain a much higher return on your capital invested is really a 'no-brainer'.

Power of reinvesting dividends

If you really want to turbocharge your share investment for maximum gain, you need to re-invest your dividends. You can do this in one of two ways:

1. If you get a cash dividend, arrange to have it directly deposited into your share trading account. When you have a reasonable amount of money in the account, buy shares — either more shares of the ones you already own and that have been performing well, or buy other shares that aren't currently in your portfolio.

2. Join the dividend reinvestment plan (DRP) if there's one. This is virtually the same as purchasing more of the shares you already own but it saves you the hassle of arranging the trades.

Joining a DRP has several other benefits:

- You can obtain shares in relatively small parcels.

- You don't need to pay brokerage.

- You avoid the temptation of spending the dividend because you don't actually get it in cash.

- You may receive your new shares at a discount price and over the years this will boost your investment even further.

- You're effectively cost-averaging the cost of your shares. (I discuss this in greater detail in the section 'Averaging', later in this chapter.)

Mind you, not everyone agrees that joining a DRP is a good idea. My position has been the same over many years and I've always preferred to re-invest the dividend into more shares rather than taking it out in cash. Because I'm a long-term investor, over the years my shareholding has grown considerably, even though I haven't bought any more shares.

> ## Tip
> Reinvesting dividends is a great way of turbocharging your share investment because you get a double whammy effect—by obtaining an extra dividend on the reinvested one.

An example from my own investing shows this clearly. I set up a self-managed super fund less than 10 years ago and invested some funds in bank shares. I joined the DRP for these shares, and the results in terms of the number of shares I now own are shown in table 12.2.

Table 12.2: Effect of the DRP on number of shares owned after 10 years

Share	Number purchased	Number I now hold
BEN	1942	2914
CBA	1986	2637
SUN	1667	2355
WBC	1942	2961

You can see how the number of shares grew significantly from reinvested dividends, even though I bought no more shares.

Total shares return

Calculating the dollar growth in value of your shares if you reinvest dividends gives you a true sense of the total return possible from shares. To calculate this, I've assumed that with the benefit of franking you can get a total dividend return of around 5%. Add this to the 7% average annual capital growth of shares in the last 40 years, and your total return from share investing should be about 12%. Based on this scenario, the value of your share investment of $10000 after a number of years is shown in table 12.3.

Table 12.3: Total return on shares over the long term.

Year	Value
5	17600
10	31100
20	96500
30	299600

After just five years, your $10 000 has grown to $17 600 and at the end of 30 years it's nearly $300 000 — even though you didn't contribute any more money to the investment! Figure 12.2 provides a visual impression of these values. I've also shown the growth lines for a 7% and 3% compound growth.

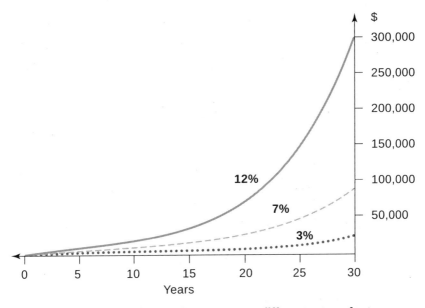

Figure 12.2: Growth of $10 000 investment at different rates of return.

These returns clearly show that if you want to turbocharge your share investment and take maximum advantage of the 'power of compounding', you need to do the following:

- get as high a return as you can

- reinvest dividends

- invest for the long term.

Rule of 72

The *Rule of 72* is an easy rule to help you work out the compound interest effect without any complex maths. The rule says that to work out the number of years for your investment to double, you divide 72 by the % annual rate.

For example, suppose you can get 7.2% return on your investment. The Rule of 72 says that the number of years needed for your investment to double is:

$$72 \div 7.2 = 10 \text{ years}$$

If you can get 10% return, your investment will double in $72 \div 10 = 7.2$ years.

If you can get 12% return, your investment will double in $72 \div 12 = 6$ years.

Varied portfolio

As I discuss way back in chapter 1, risk and return are closely related. It follows that if you want to get higher returns from shares, you need to take a higher risk. Also, as I discuss in chapter 5, the level of risk you're comfortable with depends on many factors, including your age, gender and stage of life. If you're comfortable with a higher risk level, you may be able to turbocharge your portfolio by including some more speculative types of shares because these have the potential to produce high capital gains if you can pick some good winners.

Another factor that helps you to boost your capital gains with these types of shares is that they're invariably cheaper and, therefore, small price rises can produce higher returns on capital invested. Remember that the return on capital invested is the real criterion of profitability. For example, say a share's price rises by 10¢ during the day's trading. If the share was trading for 50¢ prior to the rise, the 10¢ rise gives you a 20% return on capital in just one day! Of course, this is terrific and we would all love to get it. But if the share price was $5 prior to the rise, the same rise of 10¢ is only a 2% return on capital. If the share was a $20 one, the 10¢ rise is only a paltry 0.5%.

A low-value share can also rise dramatically in price over a longer period and so produce very high capital gain. For example, a 10¢ speckie could be worth $1.00 in a year or so if there's some fulfilment of the blue sky potential. So if you invested $1000 initially, the parcel value would rise to $10 000 and you would be showing a profit of $9000 on your initial investment of $1000! This type of scenario is certainly possible and occurs reasonably often with some speculative shares. However, this scenario is extremely unlikely with a high-priced blue chip share. Could you see Commonwealth

Bank shares, worth about $100 at the time of writing, being worth $1000 each in a year or so? I think you'd agree this is highly unlikely.

A good and less risky alternative to direct investment in more speculative shares is a listed investment company, managed fund or trust where the investment style is biased toward high capital growth. These funds or trusts may be called 'growth', 'emerging companies', 'small caps' or some similar name. Some may include overseas investments in growing economies or in emerging businesses offering good opportunities for capital growth.

Tip

With the more speculative types of share investments, the risk of loss is higher—so I suggest you don't allocate too much of your investment capital to these.

Averaging

As you know, share prices don't rise or fall in nice straight lines. Instead, lots of hills and dales occur along the way. A strategy you can use to help you smooth out the lumps and bumps—and so increase overall returns—is known as *cost or price averaging*. You use cost averaging with purchases and price averaging with sales.

To show you how cost averaging works, suppose you have about $5000 in your kitty. You've been watching some shares thinking now could be a good time to buy them. Their present price is $2.40, but the price has been rather choppy and you're not certain if you should jump in now or wait awhile. If you use cost averaging, you split the purchase so you don't commit all your funds at once. For example, you could buy 1030 shares now at $2.40, giving a parcel cost of $2492 (with $20 brokerage). You can then watch and wait to see what develops. If the price rises and confirms your opinion of the shares, you can then buy another parcel. Let's suppose the price rises to $2.60, so now you buy another 950 shares at $2.60, giving a parcel cost of $2490 including brokerage. You now have a total of 1980 shares that have cost you $4982, so the average cost of each share is about $2.52.

Suppose after you buy your first parcel, your fears are realised and the price instead falls. If you've made 10% your maximum loss target, when the price falls to $2.16, you'll sell. In this case, you sell 1030 shares at $2.16 receiving $2205 net (after brokerage). Your loss will be $287 ($2492 – $2205). But if you'd gone ahead and spent your $5000 on the first parcel, you would have initially purchased 2075 shares. When the price fell to $2.16 and you sold, you'd receive $4462 net and your loss would be $538. So by cost averaging you've cut the loss almost in half.

You can see that cost averaging a purchase is a two-edged sword. If the price rises after your first purchase, you won't make as much profit but if the price falls, you won't lose as much.

You can use the same strategy with selling, where it's known as price averaging. Instead of selling all your shares in one parcel, you sell some immediately and then wait to see what develops. If the price falls further, you can sell the remainder, but if the price rises, you don't sell and wait to see how far the price rises. If it reaches a peak and starts to fall, you can sell at this point and make more profit than you would have had you sold all your shares initially.

The beauty of cost and price averaging is that these strategies buy you some time and give you some elbow room to manoeuvre. It's a bit like having insurance on your trades, because these strategies reduce the risk. If your trade goes in the opposite direction from what you thought it would, these strategies reduce your loss. However, as mentioned, if you originally pick the price direction correctly, you won't make as much profit. These strategies also increase your trading cost, but this shouldn't amount to much if you're trading online.

Tip

If the shares you're thinking of trading have a substantial value, you can cost or price average in more than two parcels.

Averaging down

While cost averaging is often a good strategy, you shouldn't use it when a share price is falling—that is, you shouldn't cost average *down*. A saying that applies to this situation is, 'Don't try to catch a falling knife'.

When you've bought some shares and the price has fallen, you might be tempted to buy some more at the lower price — with the idea of cost averaging a lower price. For example, say you have some shares in your portfolio you purchased for $2.50. As you keep tabs on them, you note with dismay that the price is falling. You hang on because you have confidence in the company and you're fairly sure the shares will recover. But they don't and soon fall to $2.00. At this point you

think, *If I bought some more now, my average price will be only $2.25 so the share price doesn't need to rise as much before I'll be making a profit.* This is almost always a bad idea. You shouldn't try to make up for a loss purchase by buying more shares at the lower price. In other words, 'Don't try to catch a falling knife'.

Tip

Averaging down is almost always a bad idea but if you're confident that a falling trend has stopped and has been replaced by an uptrend that will be sustained, by all means buy some more shares at the lower price.

Momentum

In the physical world, momentum is possessed by bodies in motion. When a body starts moving due to a push, it won't slow down and stop until an opposing force is applied to it. That's why we have brakes on a car and why aircraft need thrust reversers.

Strange to say, but momentum has a very similar meaning with shares. A share price languishing in the doldrums won't get moving unless some force propels it. On the other hand, when a share price gets moving, it tends to keep going in the same way. The main reason for this is that investors tend to 'follow the herd' and go with the flow once a trend starts.

The important point about momentum with shares is that when a share price gets into a trend, it often goes too far before the trend changes. Recognising this with a price uptrend is particularly important, because once the trend becomes established, a price often rises way above a fair valuation before commonsense reasserts itself and the price falls and stabilises at a more realistic value. This effect of momentum on an uptrend is shown in figure 12.3.

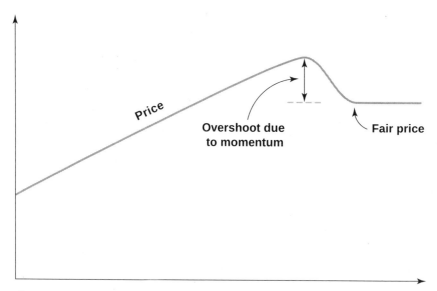

Figure 12.3: Overshoot due to momentum

Tip

Don't get sucked into an uptrend when the share price rises way above a fair valuation. The high price will seldom be sustained—simply because it can't be justified.

Dead cat bounce

Another occurrence related to share price movements is also worth keeping an eye out for because it's quite common. When an object falls from a height and strikes a hard ground surface, it will bounce a little before coming to rest. If the object were an animal, the fall would most likely kill or severely injure it. However, if a cat falls from a height, it has the ability to turn while falling, land on its feet and bounce up unharmed. But if a dead cat falls, it can't do this—but it will still bounce a little when striking the hard ground surface. With share price trends this small bounce is rather gruesomely known as a *dead cat bounce*.

The relevance to the sharemarket is when a share price has been in a downtrend for some time, it can seem to hit bottom and then start rising again. Many investors take this bounce as a sign that the downtrend has ended and is being replaced by a new uptrend. They rush to buy the shares, expecting to make good profits as the price rises. But the bounce is often only a temporary one and, before long, the price heads south again. Needless to say, investors who jumped in too soon end up making a loss. This temporary bounce is an example of a dead cat bounce because it's only a small bounce and not a true change in trend, as shown in figure 12.4.

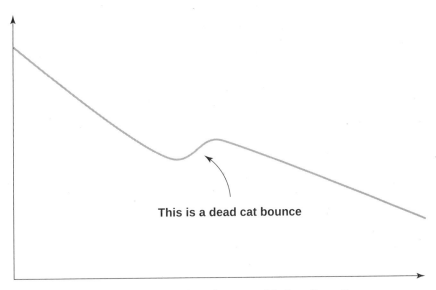

This is a dead cat bounce

Figure 12.4: Apparent recovery in a downtrend before it continues

In this type of situation, the trick is to try to distinguish a genuine trend change that will be sustained from a dead cat bounce that won't be. A good way of doing this is to not jump in immediately should a share price start to recover after being in a downtrend for some time. Instead, wait awhile to see if the uptrend is sustained and a true trend change, or if it's just a dead cat bounce. Also use your knowledge of charting and look at the share price chart with a moving average. If the moving average starts to rise after falling, this usually provides good confirmation of a definite trend change.

Tip

For the purpose of verifying a genuine downtrend change and avoiding the dead cat bounce, use a fairly short-term moving average—in the range of 10 to 20 days. Although a longer term moving average provides more reliable confirmation, you're likely to miss most of the profit because it will take too long for the trend change to be confirmed by the change in the moving average.

Applying principles (rules) to boost returns

I outline some very important principles of share investing in chapter 5—in fact, they are so important I called them *Golden Rules*. I'm now going to give you an example of three of these rules in action to show you how powerful they can be in helping you to make share investing profitable.

The three rules I'm going to use are:

1. Make rational decisions (be dispassionate and don't let emotion sway your decisions).

2. Limit losses but let profits run.

3. Practise good diversification.

In this example, you decide to invest in shares and deposit $50 000 in your share trading account. You've read my book and decide to practise good diversification, so you buy five different shares with this cash (well done)!

Let's call these shares A, B, C, D and E. You buy $10000 worth of each of these shares so at the start of the year you have five shares in your portfolio and no cash left.

For the purpose of this example, I'm going to assume that overall the market is flat and while some shares rise in price, others fall by the same amount. For the moment I won't consider trading costs.

Let's consider two possible strategies:

- *Strategy 1:* Buy and hold.

- *Strategy 2:* Limit losses but let profits run.

Table 12.4 shows the end of year (EOY) result from following strategy 1, or the buy and hold strategy.

Table 12.4: Returns after one year from following a buy and hold strategy

Share	Initial value	Performance	Action	Profit/loss	EOY value
A	$10000	Up 35%	Hold	$3500	$13500
B	$10000	Up 15%	Hold	$1500	$11500
C	$10000	No change	Hold	$0	$10000
D	$10000	Down 15%	Hold	-$1500	$8500
E	$10000	Down 35%	Hold	-$3500	$6500
Total	$50000		Total	$0	$50000

You can see from table 12.4 that if you use a buy and hold strategy, you end the year the same as you started, with the rises and falls balancing one another. You still have shares to the value of $50000 and no cash in your account. Actually you'll have made a loss of $100 because you've traded 5 times at a cost of $20 per trade.

Let's now see what happens if you abandon the buy and hold strategy and instead use strategy 2—limiting losses but letting profits run. That's to say, if the price rises, you'll continue to hold, but should the price fall by 10% or more, you'll sell.

I think you'll agree this isn't a very complicated or difficult strategy; in fact, it's a very simple one. It's also realistic because a 10% stop loss is a practical level you can set and adhere to.

Table 12.5 shows you the EOY result of applying this strategy to the same portfolio.

Table 12.5: Returns after one year from limited losses and letting profits run.

Share	Initial value	Performance	Action	Profit/loss	EOY value
A	$10 000	Up 35%	Hold	$3500	$13 500
B	$10 000	Up 15%	Hold	$1500	$11 500
C	$10 000	No change	Hold	$0	$10 000
D	$10 000	Down 15%	Sell at 10% down	–$1000	0
E	$10 000	Down 35%	Sell at 10% down	–$1000	0
Total	$50 000		Total	$3000	$35 000

After one year, you now have a portfolio of three shares with a total value $35 000. However, the two shares you sold reaped $9000 each, and so you deposited $18 000 in your trading account during the year. So at the end of the year, the total value of your shares plus cash in your account is $53 000. In other words, even though the market was flat for the year, with rises and falls balancing one another, you've managed to end the year with a profit of $3000. Well done! Actually your capital gains profit will be about $2860 because you traded seven times at a cost of $20 per trade. However, if you used another of my golden rules and bought shares that paid a dividend, you should also have some dividend income in addition to capital gains and these will offset the trading costs.

From this example, you can see that even in a flat market you can make a capital gains profit from your shares if you use the strategy I suggest. In fact, you can even make a capital gains profit from your portfolio in a falling market provided that a few of your shares are good winners!

Good money management

In this section, I explain another very important strategy that will help you turbocharge your share investment. The strategy is based on good money management and the principle of not risking more than a small proportion of your investing capital on any one share. If you have a reasonably diversified portfolio, you can apply good money management using a 2% loss rule:

Don't lose more than 2% of your investing capital on any one share.

Let's see how this rule works.

Consider my previous example where you had $50 000 invested in five different shares with $10 000 invested in each.

Now, 2% of your investing capital of $50 000 is $1000. If you're going to apply the 2% loss rule, you should not lose more than $1000 on any one share. Because each share parcel has a value of $10 000, $1000 is 10% of the shares' value. So should any share drop in value by 10%, you can sell it and not lose more than 2% of your total capital and so abide by the rule. You can do this with no problems by setting a 10% stop loss or just placing a sell order should the share price drop by 10%.

If you have a more diversified portfolio of, say, 10 different shares you can use a lower risk rule. You can even use a 1% loss rule, meaning you aren't going to risk more than 1% of your capital on any one share. I think you'll agree that this isn't very much.

If your investing capital was $50 000, for example, and you had 10 different shares in your portfolio, each would have a value of $5000. So to apply the 1% loss rule, you don't want to risk more than $500 on any one share. You can do this and still use a 10% stop loss because 10% of $5000 is $500. Therefore, you can see that with a portfolio of 10 shares, you can set a realistic 10% stop loss limit on any one share and not risk more than 1% of your total capital should the share price dive.

Tip

No matter the overall value of your portfolio, if you have 10 shares or more in it, you can use the lower 1% loss rule and still apply a 10% stop loss limit with each share.

Key takeaways

- Compounding is a mathematical principle you can take advantage of to turbocharge your share investment.

- Deciding whether to invest in a low-yielding and low-growth asset such as a bank deposit or shares is really a no-brainer. With a bank deposit your invested money is unlikely to even keep up with inflation!

- To get the benefit of compounding, you need to invest over the longer term and reinvest your profits instead of withdrawing them. This includes reinvesting dividends.

- Joining the DRP (if there is one) is the easiest way of reinvesting your dividends.

- The *Rule of 72* is an easy way to compare different investments with compound returns.

- Speculative types of shares offer the possibility of a high capital gains profit but the risk is higher, so don't devote too much of your capital to them.

- Multi-parcel trading allows you to apply cost averaging to purchases and price averaging to sales. This buys you some time so you can see what develops without committing all your funds at once. But you shouldn't try to average down and catch a falling knife.

- A very important method of minimising losses with shares is good money management. When you do this, you ensure that the possible loss on any one share doesn't exceed a small proportion of your invested capital.

- With a portfolio of five shares, you can use a 2% loss rule with a 10% stop loss limit; with a portfolio of 10 shares or more, you can use the lower 1% loss rule.

Chapter 13

Let's recap

I've given you a lot to think about through this book, especially if you're new to shares. In this last chapter, I don't introduce anything new. Instead, I reinforce the important points I suggest you remember, and summarise the most important aspects of trading you can apply to improve your success with shares.

Important points to remember

Some important points are worth really cementing in your mind. I remind you of these basics in this section.

Trust yourself

Right at the start of this journey, I asked you to trust yourself because I believe you have the necessary nous to be able to make a success of share investing. After reading through the book and gaining the knowledge you need, I'd like to think you now feel more confident about share investing. You don't need to adopt complex strategies or pay a financial advisor or subscribe to some super-duper system or computer program to be successful.

Share investing isn't an exact science. Predicting how shares will perform is a leap into the future, and no-one can predict the future with

'I can do this!'

any degree of certainty. So trust yourself—you're just as likely to make good decisions as anyone else.

Of course, not all your share investments will be profitable, and you'll probably look back at times and think, *I wish I hadn't bought these shares* or *I wish I hadn't sold these shares.* In these situations, try to work out if you did anything wrong and, if you did, how you can avoid making this mistake in the future. Then dust yourself off, pick yourself up and get on with your share investing.

Tip

If you're still not feeling very confident, try starting out with shares in a small way so you can test the water. You don't have to jump in 'boots and all' right from the start.

Choose simplicity rather than complexity

Thinking that the more complex your share investing system, the more profit you'll make is a mistake. Some very simple systems can be just as profitable as the very complex ones. No system will work well in all situations and there's no magic bullet. If you have a choice, go for simplicity rather than complexity.

Look forward

Share investors look towards the future because future profits can't be made from past results. Remember my analogy from chapter 5 of share investing being like driving a car—a good driver should glance in the rear-view mirror from time to time but most of the time should be looking forward. Shares are the same—the past provides a guide only and the future is what's important.

An investor and a trader are different

I urge you to consider yourself an investor rather than a trader. Investors take a long-term view and set up a portfolio of quality shares. Traders take a short-term view and want to make quick profits from short-term changes in the share price and so trade more speculative and risky types of shares.

Choose quality shares

I've used the term *quality* throughout the book to describe shares that are of the blue chip type. These shares are best for longer term investing because their price is unlikely to fall unexpectedly and is more likely to rise over the years. Quality companies should be making a profit and the earnings should be growing (or at least not falling). They should also pay a reasonable dividend (usually fully franked). Shares in these companies are more stable and less risky than the more speculative types of shares.

Have core shares and satellites

I suggest your portfolio should consist of a mix of core and satellite shares, with most of your capital invested in the core. The core should consist of quality shares and you shouldn't need to trade them too often (if at all). The satellites are the more speculative types of shares that offer the possibility of higher capital gains in the shorter term. They probably won't provide any dividend income and, no doubt, you'll need to trade them more often.

Profit (or earnings) is king

The most important factor in any business is profit—also known as *earnings*. For a shareholder, an important earnings statistic is the *earnings per share* (EPS). This is the total earnings of the business divided by the number of its shares on issue. The EPS can be related to the share price by another important statistic known as the *price to earnings ratio* (PE). This is the share price divided by the EPS.

The PE tells you the number of years it would take to pay for a share from the earnings attributed to it. The PE of Australian shares is usually around 20, and this is a good benchmark value you can use. If the PE of a share is much higher than this, profit per share is low in comparison to the price; that is, the shares are expensive. The price of these types of shares is high because investors build an element of blue sky potential for higher future profits into the price. Low PE shares are 'cheaper', which implies that the shares aren't valued highly by investors—most likely because they think the potential for future growth in profits is low.

If a quality share falls on hard times and business profits fall, the share price will also fall. The company may get to the point of being regarded as a 'fallen angel'. Whether the share price will rise again depends on how investors rate the prospects of recovery and likely profit growth. If a speculative share doesn't achieve the promise of future profitability and investors become disenchanted with it, the share price will fall and eventually the shares could become worthless.

Tip

In some cases, the PE of a quality share can be a fair bit higher than the benchmark value I suggested. The reason is that, in addition to the blue sky potential, investors rate the shares highly—most likely because of steady growth in EPS over the years. For example, at the time of writing blue chip CSL shares had a PE of around 35.

Capital is important in a business

Capital is the term used for money in a business. Without capital, a business can't function. A business initially gets capital from its shareholders, known as *equity capital*. The business can also obtain capital by means of a loan from a financial institution, known as *loan capital*. A certain amount of loan capital is desirable but a business with too much loan capital becomes vulnerable to any downturn in the economy and, therefore, is a more risky proposition.

As the business gets going, it should make a profit and some of this profit should be retained and reinvested back into the business as reserves, so in time the amount of capital the business has should increase. If the business can't make a profit, it needs to keep drawing on its capital pool. Eventually, it will run out of capital and become bankrupt. Many listed Australian companies don't make a profit and they're a more risky proposition—so I feel they're not really suitable for your core portfolio.

Profiting from shares

You can profit from shares in two ways:

1. *Capital gains:* The profit you make from selling after a share price has risen.

2. *Dividends:* The profit you obtain from recurring payouts.

Capital gains

You make a capital gain from shares when you sell them at a higher price than you bought them. You don't make a true capital gain or loss until you sell. For shares you own, your capital gain or loss is just a 'paper' profit or loss; it doesn't provide any real income and isn't taxable. If you decide to sell shares you've held for a year or more, only half the capital gain is taxable income.

Dividends

You get dividend income when you hold shares in a business and the directors make a payment to shareholders. The important statistic for you is the *dividend per share* (DPS). The more shares you have, the greater the dollar dividend amount you'll receive.

Another important dividend statistic is the *yield*, which is the DPS divided by the share price and expressed as a percentage. The yield is equivalent to interest and, at the time of writing, you could consider a reasonable yield to be around 3% or so.

Some companies have a dividend reinvestment plan (DRP) that allows you to take your dividend in shares rather than cash. Dividend income is taxable regardless of whether you receive it in cash or shares. If the dividend is franked, you get a refund from the tax office for the franking (or imputation) credits associated with the dividend. These are credit for the tax already paid by the company on the profit out of which the dividend was paid. The higher the franking, the higher your tax credits, so it's beneficial to have shares that are fully franked or highly franked. You can compare shares with different levels of franking using a *grossing-up factor*. For a fully franked dividend this factor is about 1.43, which means that a 4% fully franked dividend is as valuable to you as a 5.72% unfranked one (4 × 1.43).

Capital gains and dividends

The best situation for you as a share investor is that the core of your portfolio consists of quality shares where you get both types of profit. The share price rises so you get a capital gain and you also periodically receive a dividend. You can expect to get an average return of about 12% pa on these types of shares, comprising 7% capital gain and 5% grossed-up dividend.

Return on investment

The real criterion of the profitability of an investment isn't just the profit in dollars but rather the *return on investment*. The return on investment is the dollar profit divided by the capital invested and expressed as a percentage per year (pa). For example, a shareholder saying they made a $10 000 profit on their shares really means very little unless you know the time period and the value of their portfolio. If the portfolio had a value of $100 000, the return is a respectable 10%, but on a $500 000 portfolio, it's a paltry 2%. If the time period was longer than a year, the equivalent return pa would be less. For example, over two years the % return pa would be half the return in one year.

It's important to note that the capital invested isn't the dollar amount *originally* invested but the *current* dollar value of the investment. If your portfolio grows in value over time (which it should), the dollar profit you make each year needs to increase as time goes on — otherwise, the return on your share investment would be falling.

Tip

Return on capital invested is important for you as an investor because it's the real measure of the profitability of your share investment. It's also important for a business so you should check the return on capital (ROC) when researching shares for your core portfolio.

Power of compounding

When you take a long-term view with your shares, you can get a great boost to your profits if you're able to tap into the power of compounding. This is the benefit you get from not cashing in profits (either dividends or capital gains) but reinvesting them. If you do this, each year the reinvested profits add to the value of your shares—so the following year the percentage return is on a higher value portfolio.

As time goes on, the compounding effect increases your portfolio value dramatically. Therefore, if you really want to boost the value of your shares over time, you need to resist the temptation of spending your profits and instead reinvest them. If you're in a DRP, your dividend is automatically reinvested; if you get a cash dividend, you need to deposit it into your trading account. When you have a reasonable balance in the account, you can buy some more shares. With capital gains all you need to do is to hold onto the shares and not sell any of them.

Using fundamental analysis

Fundamental analysis is where you really get to know a business before you invest in it. You should focus on two types of fundamentals: general and financial. General fundamentals include factors such as the nature of the business (including the sector it's in), the size of the business, the number of years it's been in operation, its products and whether they're in the form of goods or services, the competition and the future outlook. Financial fundamentals are the aspects accountants are concerned with, such as the amount of capital, the dollar profit, the value of the assets owned by the business and its liabilities.

Tip

Before you consider a share as a candidate for inclusion in your core portfolio, you really need to have a good idea about the business and its prospects for future profitability.

Charting to time your trades

Charting is also known as *technical analysis* and it can help you to detect *trends*—that is, prolonged movements upward, downward or sideways. Apart from trend recognition, charts are a very useful aid to help you to time your trades and decide if now is a good time to buy or sell. The most reliable trading strategy is to buy in an uptrend and sell in a downtrend. Expressed the other way, don't buy in a downtrend or sell in an uptrend (unless you really need the cash).

The most common chart is the price chart but volume is also often shown as a bar chart below the price chart. The general rule is that price moves on large volumes are more significant than price moves on small ones.

Obtaining and customising charts

The best method of obtaining charts is from the internet and if you're using an online broker, their site usually includes charting software. The chart will often be interactive, meaning you're able to customise it in various ways. The default time period of a chart is usually one year but if you can change this, you can use a longer term chart for longer term trend identification and a shorter term one for more recent trends.

You may also be able to vary the way prices are shown; the most common ways are the line chart and the bar type, such as the OHLC chart and candle chart. I find candle charts are best for shorter term charts, and OHLC charts or line charts better for longer term ones.

Detecting trends

The difficulty of detecting trends is that share prices often change each day as buyers and sellers interact, and this causes short-term price movements known as *scatter* or *noise*. These tend to mask the overall trend. To help you to identify the underlying trend from the short-term scatter, most charting software allows you to show a moving average on the chart. Several types of moving average are available, with the most common ones being the simple moving average (SMA) and exponential moving average (EMA). While there's a big difference in how they're calculated, there's not a great deal of difference in their ability to identify trends.

You can usually vary the term of the moving average, with a shorter term average being more sensitive but less reliable than a longer term one. If you can show two moving averages on the same chart, their crossover points can provide good trading signals. The shorter term one crossing above the longer term one as the price is trending upward is known as a *golden cross* and is a buy signal, whereas the shorter term one crossing below the longer term one as the price is trending downward is called a *dead cross* and is a sell signal.

Tip

If you have a choice of moving averages, I suggest you use the EMA because it's a little more sensitive to recent price changes.

Trading

By far the most common way of getting into shares is by purchasing them from a shareholder who wants to sell shares they own. The act of buying or selling shares on the market is known as *trading*. A new public company issues shares by *floating* and, in this case, you can obtain their shares before they're traded on the market by filling out an application form in the prospectus and paying the required amount. This is also known as an *IPO* (initial public offering). It's also possible to inherit shares or obtain them from a demutualisation but these are relatively rare ways of becoming a shareholder.

Using a broker

You can't trade directly on the market and you need the services of a broker. The two types of broker are offline and online. An offline broker is a person you can talk with to discuss your trading plans and who will trade on your behalf. Offline brokers usually offer several types of service, varying from full service down to a no-advice broker. Naturally, the fees vary according to the level of service you require. An online broker maintains a trading website that you can use for share trading if you're an approved customer. The site usually has lots of information about shares and also a charting facility. Using an online broker has many advantages and they're the lowest cost way of trading, but the downside is that you can't discuss your planned trades with a knowledgeable person at the online site.

Types of order

When you're ready to trade, many share trading orders are possible, with the most common ones being limit orders, market orders and deferred execution orders. With limit orders, you state a price limit; with market orders, you accept the current market price. Deferred execution orders are more complex because you need to specify a trigger price as well as a limit price. The most common deferred execution order you may want to use is the stop loss order, designed to limit your loss should the share price fall substantially. However, in some cases (such as sudden price gaps down), a stop loss order may be ineffectual so the protection isn't guaranteed.

Trading plan

Before you trade any shares, having a trading plan for both purchase and selling trades—and preferably one that's written down—is a good idea. Your trading plan outlines your reasons for wanting to trade the shares in question, the type of trade, trade price, number of shares and parcel value. Your plan should also contain an exit strategy in case shares you've purchased don't meet your expectations.

Managing psychological factors

Taking emotion out of the decisions and actions you need to take with shares is very difficult. But being aware of them can help to manage them.

Fear of loss (FOL)

Everyone likes to win and no-one likes to lose. You don't actually make a loss with a share that falls in value until you sell, so FOL shows itself as a reluctance to sell a losing share. As I've already mentioned, when you're making a loss you need to swallow the bitter pill and take the necessary action and sell. Try to regard the sell transaction as just another trade.

Fear of missing out (FOMO)

No-one likes to miss out on a good thing. When you feel everyone else is making a motza with shares, resisting the temptation to join in and become a winner too is difficult. The danger is that when people get enthusiastic about shares, their optimism can drive prices to unrealistic levels. This is also known as the momentum effect (as covered in chapter 12). Of course, you should ride winners. But at the same time, don't let FOMO sway you into buying overpriced shares without rational analysis to confirm that the high price is justified.

Confirmation bias

Always wanting to be right—and not admitting to ourselves or others when we get it wrong—is another human failing. This can result in a confirmation bias, where we take on board any evidence that seems to support our convictions and disregard any evidence that contradicts them. For example, we may purchase a share because we're convinced it's going to be a winner. We then expectantly wait for our faith to be justified. If we get good news about the share, we take it on board and this reinforces our original conviction. On the other hand, if we get bad news we tend to ignore it, using all sorts of cop-out reasons to justify why we think this news is irrelevant. This bias is also called *blinkered vision* or *looking at things through rose-coloured glasses*, and it's a trap you should try to avoid.

Tip

Being able to recognise the psychological factors I've mentioned can help you to avoid letting them unduly influence your share investing decisions.

'I need to cut free if I'm going to fly high.'

Managing your portfolio

Your share portfolio is the total of all the shares you own. While setting up a good portfolio is certainly important, managing it as time goes on is even more important. In fact, I believe good portfolio management is the most important aspect of successful share investing.

Managing your portfolio involves keeping up to date with the shares in it (a process known as *monitoring*), periodically reviewing your portfolio and deciding if some change is needed. You can consider several actions after reviewing:

- Do nothing.

- Place stop-loss orders on any shares that look iffy so you can be protected if their price falls, or set yourself a price limit and sell should the price fall to that limit.

- Identify shares that need close watching because you may need to take some action in the near future.

- Re-jig your portfolio by adding some new shares and perhaps selling some existing ones.

Deciding which of these possible actions you should take isn't easy — especially if you realise selling some of your shares would be best, but by doing so you'll be locking in a loss. If you conclude that you really should take some action, you need to act. All that monitoring and reviewing and deciding something needs to be done is pointless unless you actually do it. It's human nature to defer acting on difficult decisions, with thoughts along the lines of, *Things could change if I wait a while.* From my experience, procrastinating is generally not a good strategy once you conclude that you really need to do something — do it now (or as soon as you can)!

Tip

Taking action on shares that aren't performing might be easier if you bear in mind that you can always sell and buy back later if the shares recover and get into an uptrend. With this strategy, you'll be up for additional brokerage but if you trade online, that won't be much.

Adopt a realistic mindset

When you purchase quality shares, they're highly likely to turn out to be a good long-term investment. With more speculative types of shares, you can be less confident, because the risk is higher that the trade might not work out as you planned. It's worthwhile remembering that you can't buy shares unless someone else wants to sell them, and you can't sell shares unless someone else wants to buy them. So someone else is most likely taking the opposite viewpoint to yours.

This means you really need to adopt a realistic mindset (especially with speculative trades), where you consider the possible downside and not just focus on what you think could be the probable upside.

Keep a cool head during market downturns

At times, the sharemarket takes a dive due to some unexpected external change, such as the COVID-19 pandemic. Fortunately, these occasions are relatively rare. If they occur, panicking and trying to get out of shares quickly is really not a good idea. Selling all your shares and trying to get back into the market later on is rarely a profitable exercise. In situations that adversely affect the whole market, the best strategy is almost always to keep a cool head, maintain a long-term outlook and simply ride out the storm without panicking.

'I'll ride out this storm without panicking.'

Practise good money management

Good money management is essential for success with shares. You can practise good money management if you diversify your investment and limit possible losses on any one share to only a small amount of your portfolio value. If you have a portfolio of five shares of roughly equal value, you can use a 2% loss rule with a 10% loss limit on any single share. In other words, if a share turns out to be a loser, you sell if the price drops by 10% so this loss will be only 2% of your portfolio value. If you have a portfolio of 10 shares (or more), you can use an even safer 1% loss rule with the same downside loss limit of 10% on any one share.

Key takeaways

I don't want to bore you by repeating the key points, so I'll conclude this chapter by re-stating my Golden Rules:

- *Golden Rule 1:* Use rational decision-making — try to base your share decisions on evidence and rational considerations rather than emotions or instincts.

- *Golden Rule 2:* Limit your losses but let your profits run.

- *Golden Rule 3:* Practise good money management with your share portfolio.

- *Golden Rule 4:* Diversify your share investing capital among various different types of shares.

- *Golden Rule 5:* Invest most of your capital in 'good quality' Australian-listed shares that pay a reasonable dividend — preferably fully franked.

- *Golden Rule 6:* Look toward the future with shares.

- *Golden Rule 7:* Buy shares only when the price is in an uptrend and sell them only when the price is in a downtrend. Another useful way of looking at this rule is: Don't buy in a downtrend and don't sell in an uptrend (unless you're desperate for the cash).

Go for it!

Congratulations if you've read through the book and come to the end of the journey. I hope you've enjoyed the ride and will now be able to use what you've learnt to make good profits from share investing. In this regard, I would like to give you my best wishes for continuing success.

If you have any queries or you would like to pass on any comments, I'm always happy to hear from readers. As I mention in the introduction to the book, you can contact me via email at rkinsky@bigpond.com or visit my website rogerkinskyshares.com.au.

You can do it, now go for it!

*'Now I've read the book, I'm ready
to plunge in.'*

Appendix:
Details of
my portfolio
spreadsheet

My portfolio spreadsheet has columns with the following headings from left to right across the page:

A   Name of the company

B   Code

C   Quantity (number of shares held)

D   Price

E   Value—which is quantity × price (calculated by the spreadsheet)

F   Dividend type—this can be ff (fully franked) or pf (partly franked) and also includes DRP (dividend reinvestment plan) if there is one

G   EPS—earnings per share

H   PE—price to earnings ratio (calculated by the spreadsheet and based on EPS and share price)

I   DPS—dividend per share in ¢

J   Y—percentage yield, which is DPS in ¢ ÷ Price in $ (calculated by the spreadsheet)

K   GUY—grossed-up yield (calculated by the spreadsheet according to the franking level)

L   TC—total cost, which is the total amount paid for the shares including purchasing cost and brokerage, as well as the cost of shares allocated through the DRP (if there is one)

M   Cap gain—the market value (column E) – TC (column L) (calculated by the spreadsheet)

N   Comments—such as sell or buy at a price I nominate, or 'watch', meaning keep a close eye on these shares because they're looking a bit dodgy.

Note the following with my spreadsheet:

- I don't need to change details in the EPS, DPS or TC columns each week but only after new earnings are announced, a new dividend is paid or when I buy more shares or sell some.

- The total cost (TC) is actually the 'accounting cost' and is the correct total cost for accounting or capital gains tax purposes.

- The capital gain (or loss) shown in my spreadsheet is correct for capital gains tax purposes but actually understates my true capital gain if I'm in a DRP. That's to say, I'm actually making a higher profit on these shares than my spreadsheet indicates. This comes about because the shares I receive in lieu of dividends don't actually cost me anything. I'm in the process of starting another spreadsheet where my true capital gain will be shown. You might want to do the same.

At the bottom of the spreadsheet, the total value of my shares and my total capital gains profit is shown (calculated by the spreadsheet). The percentage gain or loss compared to last week is also shown. I insert this week's value of the XAO index (All Ords) and the spreadsheet calculates the percentage gain or loss of the All Ords over the week. I can compare my portfolio gain or loss to that of the XAO, and this gives me a good indication of my portfolio performance compared to the general market.

When printed, my spreadsheet is A4 in size with portrait format. Getting all the columns in to this size paper is a bit of a squeeze, but I manage to do it so I can get a one-page printout. If you don't have too many shares you could overcome this difficulty by using the landscape format.

Index

Also available by Roger Kinsky

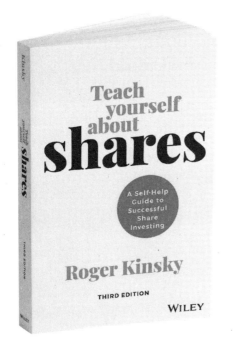

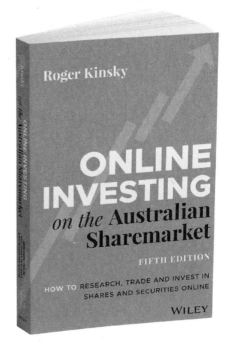

WILEY